Series / Number 07-056

INTRODUCTION TO LINEAR GOAL PROGRAMMING

JAMES P. IGNIZIO
Pennsylvania State University

SAGE PUBLICATIONS
Beverly Hills London New Delhi

For information address:

SAGE Publications, Inc.
275 South Beverly Drive
Beverly Hills, California 90212

SAGE Publications India Pvt. Ltd.
M-32 Market
Greater Kailash I
New Delhi 110 048, India

SAGE Publications Ltd
28 Banner Street
London EC1Y 8QE
England

International Standard Book Number 0-8039-2564-6

Library of Congress Catalog Card No. 85-072574

FIRST PRINTING

When citing a University paper, please use the proper form. Remember to cite the correct Sage University Paper series title and include the paper number. One of the following formats can be adapted (depending on the style manual used):

(1) IVERSEN, GUDMUND R. and NORPOTH, HELMUT (1976) "Analysis of Variance." Sage University Paper series on Quantitative Applications in the Social Sciences, 07-001. Beverly Hills: Sage Pubns.

OR

(2) Iversen, Gudmund R. and Norpoth, Helmut. 1976. *Analysis of Variance.* Sage University Paper series on Quantitative Applications in the Social Sciences, series no. 07-001. Beverly Hills: Sage Pubns.

CONTENTS

Series Editor's Introduction

As this series of volumes in quantitative applications has grown, we have begun to reach out to those in economics and business in the same way that some of the earlier volumes appealed most especially to those in political science, sociology, and psychology. Our goal, however, continues to be the same: to publish readable, up-to-date introductions to quantitative methodology and its application to substantive problems.

One of the fastest-growing areas within the fields of operations research and management science, in terms of both interest as well as actual implementation, is the methodology known as goal programming. From its inception in the early 1950s, this tool has rapidly evolved into one that now encompasses nearly all classes of multiple objective programming models. Of course, it has also undergone a significant evolution during that time.

In *An Introduction to Linear Goal Programming*, James Ignizio (a pioneer and major contributor to the field, whose first application of goal programming was in 1962 in the deployment of the antenna system for the Saturn/Apollo moon landing mission) provides a concise, lucid, and current overview of (a) the linear goal programming model, (b) a computationally efficient algorithm for solution, (c) duality and sensitivity analysis, and (d) extensions of the methodology to integer as well as nonlinear models. To accomplish this extent of coverage in a short monograph, Ignizio uses a matrix-based presentation, a format that not only permits a concise overview but one that is also most compatible with the manner in which real-world mathematical programmming problems are solved.

The text is intended for individuals in the fields of operations research, management science, industrial and systems engineering, computer science, and applied mathematics who wish to become familiar with linear goal programming in its most recent form. Prerequisites for the text are limited to some background in linear algebra and knowledge of the more elementary operations in matrices and vectors.

—*Richard G. Niemi*
Series Co-Editor

Acknowledgments

During more than two decades of research in and applications of goal programming, I have been influenced, motivated, and guided by the works and words of numerous individuals. Several of these individuals, in particular, have had a major impact. These include Abraham Charnes and William Cooper, the originators of the concept of goal programming; Veikko Jääskeläinen, an individual whose substantial impact on the present-day popularity of goal programming has been almost totally overlooked; and Paul Huss, who introduced me to goal programming, influenced my development of the first nonlinear goal programming algorithm and application (in 1962), and was my co-developer of the first large-scale linear goal programming code (in 1967). I also wish to acknowledge the influence of the text, *Advanced Linear Programming* (McGraw-Hill, 1981) by Bruce Murtagh. Murtagh's outstanding text and its concise yet lucid style have had particular influence on the presentation found in Chapter 4 of this work. Finally, particular thanks are given to Tom Cavalier and Laura Ignizio for comments and contributions to the original draft of this manuscript.

INTRODUCTION TO LINEAR GOAL PROGRAMMING

JAMES P. IGNIZIO
Pennsylvania State University

1. INTRODUCTION

Although goal programming (GP) is itself a development of the 1950s, it has only been since the mid-1970s that GP has finally received truly substantial and widespread attention. Much of the reason for such interest is due to GP's demonstrated ability to serve as an efficient and effective tool for the modeling, solution, and analysis of mathematical models that involve multiple and conflicting goals and objectives—the type of models that most naturally represent *real-world* problems. Yet another reason for the interest in GP is a result of a growing recognition that conventional (i.e., single objective) mathematical programming methods (e.g., linear programming) do not always provide reasonable answers, nor do they typically lead to a true understanding of and insight into the actual problem.

Purpose

It is then the purpose of this monograph to provide for the reader a brief but reasonably comprehensive introduction to the multiobjective mathematical programming technique known as goal programming, with specific focus on the use of such an approach in dealing with *linear* systems. Further, in providing such an introduction, we shall attempt to minimize both the amount and level of sophistication of the associated mathematics. As such, the only prerequisite for the reader is some exposure to linear algebra and a knowledge of the more elementary operations on matrices and vectors. It should be emphasized that a familiarity with linear programming has not been assumed, although it is believed likely that most readers will have had some previous work in that area. It has been my attempt to provide a brief and concise, but reasonably rigorous treatment of linear goal programming.

What Is Goal Programming?

At this point, let us pause and reflect upon some of the notions expressed above, in conjunction with a few new ideas. First, let us note that goal programming has, in itself, nothing to do with computer programming (e.g., FORTRAN, Pascal, LISP, BASIC). That is, although any GP problem of meaningful size would certainly be solved on the computer, the notion of "programming" in GP (or, for that matter, in the whole of mathematical programming) is associated with the development of solutions, or "programs," for a specific problem. Thus, the name "goal programming" is used to indicate that we seek to find the (optimal) program (i.e., set of policies that are to be implemented) for a mathematical model that is composed *solely* of goals. Linear goal programming, or LGP, in turn is used to describe the methodology employed to find the program for a model consisting solely of *linear* goals.

We shall wait until Chapter 3 to rigorously define the notion of a "goal." Here, we simply note that *any* mathematical programming model may find an alternate representation via GP. Further, not only does GP provide an alternative representation, it also often provides a representation that is far more effective in capturing the nature of real-world problems—problems that involve multiple and conflicting goals and objectives.

Finally, we note that conventional (i.e., single objective) mathematical programming may be easily and effectively treated as a subset, or special class, of GP. For example, as we shall see, linear programming models are easily and conveniently treated as "GP" models. In fact, and although the idea is considered radical by the traditionalists, it is not really necessary to study linear programming (LP) if one has a *thorough* background in LGP.

On the Use of Matrix Notation

As mentioned earlier, one of the prerequisites of this text is that the reader has had some previous exposure to matrices and vectors, and the associated notation, terminology, and basic operations employed in such areas. Although at first glance the matrix-based approach used herein may appear a bit formidable to some of the readers, be assured that its purpose is not to complicate the issue. Instead, by means of such an approach we are able to:

(1) provide a presentation that is typically clearer, more concise, and less ambiguous than if a nonmatrix-based approach were employed; and
(2) provide algorithms in a form far closer to that actually employed in developing *efficient* computerized algorithms.

Of particular importance is the conciseness provided via a matrix-based approach. Using matrices and matrix notation we are able, in this slim volume, to still cover nearly all of the useful features of linear goal programming (e.g., a reasonably computationally efficient version of an algorithm for linear goal programming, a comprehensive presentation of duality, an introduction to sensitivity analysis, and even discussions of various extensions of the methodology). Without the use of the matrix-based approach, there would have been no possibility of covering this amount of material in even two or three times the amount of pages used herein.

For those readers whose exposure to matrices and vectors has been limited, or is a part of the now distant past, there is no reason for apprehension. The level of the matrix-based presentation employed has been kept quite elementary.

2. HISTORY AND APPLICATIONS

Although there exist numerous related earlier developments, the field of mathematical programming typically is traced to the development of the general linear programming model and its most common method for solution, designated as "simplex." LP and simplex were, in turn, developed in 1947 by a team of scientists, led by George Dantzig, under the sponsorship of the U.S. Air Force project SCOOP (Scientific Computation Of Optimum Programs). The LP model addressed a *single*, linear objective function that was to be optimized subject to a set of *rigid*, linear constraints. One of the best discussions of this radical new concept is given by Dantzig himself (Dantzig, 1982).

Within but a few years, LP had received substantial international exposure and attention, and was hailed as one of the major developments of applied mathematics. Today, LP is probably the most widely known and certainly one of the most widely employed of the methods used by those in such fields as operations research and management science. However, as with *any* quantitative approach to the modeling and solution of real problems, LP has its blemishes, drawbacks, and limitations. Of these, our interest is focused on the inability—or at least limited ability—of LP to directly and effectively address problems involving *multiple* objectives and goals, subject to *soft* as well as rigid (or hard) constraints.

The development of GP—one approach for eliminating or at least alleviating the above-mentioned limitations of LP—originated in the early 1950s. At this time, Charnes and Cooper addressed a problem seemingly unrelated to LP (or GP): the problem of (linear) regression with side conditions. To solve this problem, Charnes and Cooper employed a somewhat modified version of LP and termed the approach "constrained regression" (Charnes et al., 1955; Charnes and Cooper, 1975).

Later, in their 1961 text, Charnes and Cooper described a more general version of constrained regression, one that was intended for dealing with linear models involving multiple objectives or goals. This refined approach was designated as goal programming and is the concept that underlies all present-day work and generalizations of GP.

In the same 1961 text, Charnes and Cooper also addressed the not so insignificant problem of attempting to measure the "goodness" of a solution for a multiple objective model. They proposed three approaches, all of which are still widely employed today. These approaches were each based on the transformation of all objectives into goals by means of the establishment of an "aspiration level," or "target." For example, an *objective* such as "maximize profit" might be restated as the *goal*: "Obtain x or more units of profit." Obviously, any solution to the converted model will either be under, over, or exactly satisfy the profit aspiration. Further, any profit *under* the desired x units represents an *undesirable* or *unwanted* deviation from the goal. Consequently, Charnes and Cooper proposed that we focus on the "minimization of *unwanted* deviations," a concept essentially identical to the notion of "satisficing" as proposed by March and Simon (Morris, 1964). Using this concept, Charnes and Cooper specified the following three forms of GP:

(1) Archimedean GP (also known as "minsum" or "weighted" GP): Here we seek to minimize the (weighted) sum of all unwanted, absolute deviations from the goals;

(2) Chebyshev GP (also known as "minimax" GP): Our purpose is to minimize the worst, or maximum of the unwanted goal deviations; and

(3) non-Archimedean GP (also known as "preemptive priority" GP or "lexicographic" GP): Here we seek the minimum (more precisely, the lexicographic minimum) of an *ordered vector* of the unwanted goal deviations.

It is of particular interest that LP (or any single-objective methodology) as well as Archimedean and Chebyshev GP may all be considered as *special cases of non-Archimedean GP*—and thus treated by the same general model and algorithm (Ignizio, forthcoming). As a result, in this work we focus our attention on non-Archimedean GP or, more specifically, on lexicographic linear goal programming.

In addition to describing the linear GP concept and proposing the above three measures for evaluation, Charnes and Cooper also outlined (again, in their 1961 text) algorithms for solution. Evidently, however, actual software for the implementation of such algorithms was not developed until the late 1960s. In fact, to the author's knowledge, the first computer code for GP was the one that I developed in 1962 (Ignizio, 1963, 1976b, 1979b, 1981b) for the solution of *nonlinear* GP models—more specifically, for the design of the antenna systems for the Saturn/Apollo moon landing program.

As a result of the success of the algorithm and software for nonlinear GP, or NLGP, I gained a considerable appreciation of and interest in GP. As a consequence, in 1967, when faced with a relatively large-scale LGP model (one that included the lexicographic minimum, or preemptive priority notions), I developed a computer code for lexicographic LGP as based on a suggestion by Paul Huss (personal communication, 1967). In a telephone conversation with me, Huss proposed that one solve the lexicographic LGP model as a *sequence* of conventional LP models. This suggestion was refined and software for the procedure was developed by the summer of 1967. This specific approach, which I designate as sequential goal programming (or SGP; or SLGP in the linear case), although unsophisticated,[1] resulted in a computer program capable of solving an LGP model of sizes equivalent to those solved via LP (Ignizio, 1967, 1982a; Ignizio and Perlis, 1979). In fact, until quite recently, SLGP (also known as iterative LGP or "decomposed" LGP) evidently has offered the best performance of any package for LGP (having now been supplanted by the MULTIPLEX codes for GP; Ignizio, 1983a, 1983e, 1985a, 1985b, forthcoming).

Later, in 1968 through 1969, Veikko Jääskeläinen also addressed the development of software for LGP.[2] Rather than employing the cruder SLGP approach (Jääskeläinen was unaware of our work as were we of his), Jääskeläinen employed the algorithm for lexicographic (i.e., non-Archimedean) LGP as originally outlined by Charnes and Cooper. To implement this algorithm, he modified the small and extremely elementary LP code as published in the text by Frazer (1968). The result was a simple code (e.g., it required a full tableau, employed elementary textbook pivoting operations, and lacked provisions for reinversion) capable of efficiently solving only problems of perhaps 30 to 50 variables and a like number of rows. However, inasmuch as Jääskeläinen's intent was simply to use the code on small problems as part of his investigation of the application of LGP to various areas, the elementary code proved sufficient (Jääskeläinen, 1969, 1976). (A complete discussion of this effort may be found in Jääskeläinen's 1969 work.)

One of the more intriguing aspects (and one that is both frustrating and embarrassing to the serious, knowledgeable advocates of GP) of the Jääskeläinen code for LGP is that today, this code is the most widely known and employed of all LGP software. This situation is particularly true in the case of many U.S. business schools where some investigators, even today, are under the illusion that this code represents the state of the art in LGP software. To compound the matter further, credit to Jääskeläinen for the development of the code is seldom if ever given. The one positive aspect of the situation is that the easy availability of the Jääskeläinen code (most other LGP codes—particularly those for truly large-scale models—are proprietary) helped encourage a substantially increased interest in GP.

In the late 1960s and early 1970s I continued to develop GP algorithms and software, including those for integer and nonlinear GP models (Draus et al., 1977; Harnett and Ignizio, 1973; Ignizio, 1963, 1967, 1976a, 1976b, 1976c, 1977a, 1978a, 1979a, 1979b, 1979c; Ignizio and Satterfield, 1977; Palmer et al., 1982; Wilson and Ignizio, 1977). However, a much more important contribution resulted as a consequence of my interest in duality in LGP. By the early 1970s, a relatively complete and formal exposition of this topic had resulted (Ignizio, 1974a, 1974b). The dual of the LGP model, termed the "multidimensional dual," rapidly led to the development of a complete methodology for sensitivity analysis in LGP models and in the development of substantially improved algorithms and software. As a consequence, today one has available a fairly wide selection of computationally efficient software for both linear as well as integer and nonlinear GP models (Charnes and Cooper, 1961, 1977; Charnes et al., 1975, 1976, 1979; Draus et al., 1977; Garrod and Moores, 1978; Harnett and Ignizio, 1973; Ignizio, 1963, 1967, 1974b, 1976b, 1976c, 1977a, 1978b, 1979a, 1979b, 1980b, 1981a, 1981b, 1981c, 1981d, 1982a, 1983b, 1983c, 1983d, 1983e, 1983f, 1984, 1985a, 1985b, forthcoming; Ignizio et al., 1982; Keown and Taylor, 1980; Masud and Hwang, 1981; McCammon and Thompson, 1980; Moore et al, 1980; Murphy and Ignizio, 1984; Perlis and Ignizio, 1980; Price, 1978; Taylor et al., 1982; Wilson and Ignizio, 1977). One may state, in fact, that *the performance of modern GP software is equivalent to that of the very best of the software used in the solution of conventional single objective models.*

Space does not permit a discussion of GP applications. However, we do provide a number of references that describe a variety of implementations of the methodology (Anderson and Earle, 1983; Bres et al., 1980; Campbell and Ignizio, 1972; Charnes et al., 1955, 1976; Charnes and Cooper, 1961, 1975, 1979; Cook, 1984; De Kluyver, 1978, 1979; Draus et al., 1977; Freed and Glover, 1981; Harnett and Ignizio, 1973; Ignizio, 1963, 1976a, 1976c, 1977, 1978a, 1979a, 1979c, 1980b, 1981b, 1981c, 1981d, 1983b, 1983d, 1983f, 1984; Ignizio et al., 1982; Ignizio and Daniels, 1983; Ijiri, 1965; Jääskeläinen, 1969, 1976; Keown and Taylor, 1980; McCammon and Thompson, 1980; Moore et al., 1978; Ng, 1981; Palmer et al., 1982; Perlis and Ignizio, 1980; Pouraghabagher, 1983; Price, 1978; Sutcliffe et al., 1984; Taylor et al., 1982; Wilson and Ignizio, 1977; Zanakis and Maret, 1981). Obviously, *any* problem that may be approached via mathematical programming (optimization) is a candidate for GP.

3. DEVELOPMENT OF THE LGP MODEL

In this chapter, we address the most important aspect, by far, in the GP methodology. Specifically, we describe a straightforward, rational, and systematic approach to the construction of the mathematical model that is designated as the LGP model.[3]

The purpose of any mathematical programming method is—or at least should be—to gain increased insight and understanding of the real-world *problem* under consideration. We hope to accomplish this by forming and "solving" a quantitative representation (i.e., the mathematical model) of the problem. What is too often forgotten, however, is that the numbers so derived are simply solutions to the abstract *model* and not, necessarily, solutions to the real *problem*. The purpose of the procedure to be described is to attempt to provide a mathematical model that as accurately as possible reflects the problem. In this way, we should be able to minimize the discrepancies between model and problem. However, prior to describing the modeling process, we first provide a summary of some of the notation that shall be used throughout the remainder of the monograph.

Notation

Our mathematical models shall be, for the most part, expressed in terms of matrix notation.

Matrices. A matrix is a rectangular array of real numbers. We represent the matrix via boldface, capital letters such as **A**, **D**, **I**. However, in the case of, say, a matrix composed solely of zeros, we denote this as boldface zero, or **0**.

Elements and order of a matrix. The i, j^{th} *element* of matrix **A** is designated as $a_{i,j}$. That is, $a_{i,j}$ is the element in row i and column j of **A**. The *order* of a matrix is given as $(m \times n)$ where m is the number of rows and n is the number of columns.

Special matrix types. In the monograph, we utilize several special matrix types, which include:

- $\mathbf{A}^T$ = the *transpose* of **A**;
- $\mathbf{B}^{-1}$ = the *inverse* of **B** (where, of course, **B** must be nonsingular);
- **I** = the *identity* matrix; and
- $(\mathbf{A}_1 : \mathbf{A}_2)$ = the *partition* of some matrix, say **A**.

Vectors. A vector is either an ordered column or row of real numbers. In this text, we shall assume that *all vectors are column vectors*. Thus, in the event of the need to designate a row vector, we will denote this by the transpose operator. Typically, we shall use boldface, lower case letters for a vector, such as: **a, b, x.** As mentioned, these are column vectors. Thus, $\mathbf{a}^T$, $\mathbf{b}^T$ and $\mathbf{x}^T$ would be row vectors.

Special vector types. Some of the special types of vectors used herein are:

- $\mathbf{a}_j$ = the jth column of matrix $\mathbf{A}$;
- $\left(\frac{\mathbf{v}_1}{\mathbf{v}_2}\right)$ = the partition of some vector, say $\mathbf{v}$;
- $\mathbf{c}^{(k)}$ = a vector associated with the kth set of objects of $\mathbf{c}$; and
- $\mathbf{x} \geqslant \mathbf{0}$; this indicates that the column vector $\mathbf{x}$ is nonnegative.

Elements of a vector. Typically, x_j shall represent the jth element of the vector $\mathbf{x}$. That is, the subscript shall indicate the element's position within the vector.

The Baseline Model

The first phase of the modeling process is to gain as much appreciation of the actual problem as possible. Typically, this is accomplished by observing (if possible) the problem situation, discussing the problem with those most familiar with it, and simply spending a great deal of time thinking about the problem and its possible reasons for existence and potential alternatives. Once one has gained some degree of familiarity with the problem, the next step is to attempt to develop an accurate mathematical model for problem representation.

It is in the initial development of this (preliminary) mathematical model that our approach differs from the traditional procedure. That is, rather than immediately developing a specific (and conventional) mathematical model (e.g., a linear programming model), we shall first develop an extremely general, as well as useful, problem representation: the "baseline model" (Ignizio, 1982a).

The general form of the baseline model is given below:

Find $\mathbf{x}^T = (x_1, x_2, \ldots, x_n)$ so as to[4]

$$\text{maximize } f_r(\mathbf{x}) \qquad \forall r \qquad [3.1]$$

$$\text{minimize } f_s(\mathbf{x}) \qquad \forall s \qquad [3.2]$$

$$\text{satisfy}^5 \; f_t(\mathbf{x}) \begin{matrix} \leqslant \\ = \\ \geqslant \end{matrix} b_t \qquad \forall t \qquad [3.3]$$

The components of this model then include: (a) variables (specifically, structural variables, also known as control or decision variables), (b) objectives (of the maximizing and minimizing form), and (c) goals (either "hard" or "soft"). Further, in some cases (including the case of either LP or LGP models as derived from the baseline model), an additional restriction typically exists in regard to the structural variables. Specifically, the structural variables *may* be restricted to only non-negative values; and this is written as:

$$\mathbf{x} \geq \mathbf{0} \qquad [3.4]$$

Terminology

Before proceeding further, let us first more precisely define the terminology associated with the baseline model. This terminology, as well as its differences from that used in conventional mathematical programming, plays an important part in the appreciation of LGP, or multi-objective mathematical programming in general.

Structural variable: Typically denoted as x_j, the structural variables are those problem variables over which one can exercise some control. Consequently, they are also known as control or decision variables.

Objective: In mathematical programming, an objective is a function that we seek to optimize, via changes in the structural variables. The two most common (but not the only) forms of objectives are those that we seek to maximize and those we wish to minimize (i.e., maximize or minimize their respective values). The functions in (3.1) are maximizing objectives whereas those in (3.2) are minimizing objectives.

Goal: The functions of (3.3) are goal functions. Specifically, they appear as objective functions *in conjunction with* a right-hand side. This right-hand side (e.g., b_t) is the "target value" or "aspiration level" associated with the goal.

To further clarify the last definition, that of a "goal," note first the relationship between a goal and an objective. For example, if we "wish to maximize profit," we are discussing an objective. However, if we say that we "wish to achieve a profit of $1000 or more," then we have stated a goal. Obviously, then, we may transform any objective into a goal by means of citing a specific target value ($1000 in the previous example).

Next, note that goals may be further classified as either "hard" (i.e., rigid or inflexible) or "soft" (i.e., flexible) depending upon just how firm our desire is to achieve the target value. Examine,for example, the profit goal listed as follows:

$$3x_1 + 6x_2 + x_3 \geq 1000 \qquad (\$ \text{ of profit})$$

Now, if we *absolutely must* achieve a profit of $1000 (e.g., if the firm will not survive otherwise), then this function is a hard, or rigid, or inflexible goal. Or, using the terminology of conventional mathematical programming, the expression represents a *rigid constraint*.

More likely, such a goal would not be inflexible. That is, the company may well want to have a profit of $1000 but will still survive if it is $999 . . . or $990 . . . or perhaps even less. In this case, the goal would be considered soft or flexible.

Based on these concepts and terminology, let us now consider the development of a small, simplified numerical example of a baseline model. The problem we consider involves the construction of a groundwater pumping station to provide potable water for a small country town. The site of the station is fixed, because of the availability of well water, and the only questions remaining (that we shall consider) are:

(1) Which of two types of monitoring station should be used?

(2) Which of three types of pumping machinery should be purchased?

The town wishes, of course, to minimize the total initial cost. However, as there is a high level of unemployment in the area, they also wish to maximize the number of workers gainfully employed. The data associated with this particular example is given below:

	Station Type		Pumping Machinery Type		
	A	B	I	II	III
Initial costs (in millions)	2	1.5	5	4	3.5
Number of personnel per 8-hour shift	4	6	6	10	15

To form the baseline model for this problem we first let

j = 1, 2, 3, 4, and 5 representing the subscripts associated with station type A, station type B, machinery type I, machinery type II, and machinery type III, respectively;

then letting

$$x_j = \begin{cases} 1 \text{ if alternative j is used} \\ 0 \text{ otherwise} \end{cases} \qquad [3.5]$$

we are ready to form the objectives, goals, and rigid constraints. Now, exactly one of the monitoring stations and exactly one of the pumping machinery types must be purchased. This may be expressed as

$$x_1 + x_2 \quad = 1 \qquad [3.6]$$

and

$$x_3 + x_4 + x_5 = 1 \qquad [3.7]$$

Next, consider the initial costs that are to be minimized. From the data table we can immediately construct the cost objective as

$$\text{minimize } 2x_1 + 1.5x_2 + 5x_3 + 4x_4 + 3.5x_5 \qquad [3.8]$$

Further, it is desired to maximize the number of workers gainfully employed. Again, from the data this objective is written as

$$\text{maximize } 12x_1 + 18x_2 + 18x_3 + 30x_4 + 45x_5 \qquad [3.9]$$

In addition, we may write the nonnegative conditions as

$$x_j \geq 0 \quad \text{for all j} \qquad [3.10]$$

Thus, reviewing the model we see that we have two objectives (relationships 3.8 and 3.9), two goals (relationships 3.6 and 3.7), and a set of nonnegativity conditions (3.10). However, notice that for this model the nonnegativity conditions are redundant because in (3.5) we have already restricted the structural variables to nonnegative values—

specifically, the values of either 0 or 1. As such, we may rewrite this model in the standard baseline form shown below:

$$\text{minimize} \quad 2x_1 + 1.5x_2 + 5x_3 + 4x_4 + 3.5x_5$$

$$\text{maximize} \quad 12x_1 + 18x_2 + 18x_3 + 30x_4 + 45x_5$$

$$\text{satisfy} \quad x_1 + x_2 = 1$$

$$x_3 + x_4 + x_5 = 1$$

where $x_j = 0$ or 1 for all j

Our final step in baseline model development is to indicate which of the goals are to be considered rigid. As the station must, evidently, be built, we may conclude that both goals in the above model are to be considered as rigid constraints.

In reviewing this model it should be obvious that, even though it has been simplified (e.g., yearly operating costs and salaries have been ignored), the problem still has two objectives and these objectives are in conflict. That is, the minimization of initial costs adversely affects the desire to maximize the number of workers employed, and vice versa. Further, we should note that this particular model is known as a "zero-one programming" model because of the restrictions on the structural variable values. In this text we shall mainly focus on models with strictly continuous variables. However, there are methods to solve the zero-one model as is briefly discussed in Chapter 7.

Additional Examples

Because of the (rigid) constraints on the length of this monograph, we shall not address any further baseline model examples. However, the reader desiring further details and examples may review Chapter 2 of my book *Linear Programming in Single and Multiple Objective Systems* (Prentice-Hall, 1982).

Conversion Process: Linear Programming

The baseline model of (3.1)-(3.4) represents the quantitative model that, if properly and carefully developed, is closest to representing the significant features of the corresponding real-world problem. Unfortunately, in the general case it is usually not feasible to attack directly such a model. This is because the available methods of solution are simply not yet adequate for dealing with such a general representation. As a consequence, our next step in the modeling process is to *transform* the baseline model into a "working model," by means of certain assumptions.

As many readers may be familiar with LP, let us first describe the conversion of the baseline model into an LP model. First, we cite the general form of the LP model:

Find $\mathbf{x}$ so as to

$$\text{minimize } z = \mathbf{c}^T\mathbf{x} \qquad [3.11]$$

such that:

$$\mathbf{A}\,\mathbf{x} = \mathbf{b} \qquad [3.12]$$

and

$$\mathbf{x} \geq \mathbf{0} \qquad [3.13]$$

For purpose of illustration, we have selected a form that has a *minimization* objective (i.e., function 3.11). However, if we instead wished to maximize the single objective, we would simply multiply it by negative one and then minimize the resultant objective. That is,

$$\text{maximize } z' = \mathbf{c}^T\mathbf{x}$$

is equivalent to

$$\text{minimize } z = -\mathbf{c}^T\mathbf{x}$$

Now, comparing the LP model of (3.11)-(3.13) with the baseline model of (3.1)-(3.4), it should be relatively apparent as to how the latter was converted into the former. The process itself may be summarized as follows:

Step 1: Select *one* objective from (3.1) or (3.2) and treat it as the single LP objective. Typically, this is the objective that is perceived to be of "most significance."

Step 2: Convert all remaining objectives into goals by means of establishing associated aspiration levels. That is,

$$\max f_r(\mathbf{x})$$

becomes

$$f_r(\mathbf{x}) \geq b_r$$

and

$$\min f_s(\mathbf{x})$$

becomes

$$f_s(\mathbf{x}) \leq b_s$$

where b_r and b_s are the respective aspiration levels for the two objective types.

Step 3: Treat all goals (i.e., including those as formed in step 2) as rigid constraints.

Step 4: Convert each inequality goal to an equation (by means of "slack" or "surplus" variables. (See, for example, Chapter 6 of *Linear Programming in Single and Multiple Objective Systems*, 1982.)

Although few analysts are ever trained to proceed through the above four steps in forming the LP model (i.e., they typically proceed directly to the LP model), we strongly believe that the assumptions underlying any LP model are made far more apparent via this process.

LGP Conversion Procedure: Phase One

We now consider the conversion of the baseline model into the lexicographic form (i.e., non-Archimedean or preemptive priority form) of the GP model. This model—most specifically in its linear form—is, of course, the focus of this monograph. This conversion process proceeds through two phases. The first phase consists of the following steps:

Step 1: *All* objectives are transformed into goals (in the same manner as treated above for LP). Thus, the baseline model of (3.1)-(3.4) becomes:[6]

$$f_i(x) \begin{smallmatrix}\leqslant\\=\\\geqslant\end{smallmatrix} b_i \qquad \forall i \qquad [3.14]$$

Note that each goal in (3.14), unlike LP, may be either hard or soft, as deemed appropriate for the most accurate representation of the problem being considered.

Step 2: Each goal in (3.14) is then rank ordered according to importance. As a result, the set of hard goals (i.e., rigid constraints) is

TABLE 3.1
Inclusion of Deviation Variables

Original Goal Form	*Converted Form*	*"Unwanted" Deviation Variable (the Variable to be Minimized)*
$f_i(x) \leqslant b_i$	$f_i(x) + \eta_i - \rho_i = b_i$	ρ_i
$f_i(x) \geqslant b_i$	$f_i(x) + \eta_i - \rho_i = b_i$	η_i
$f_i(x) = b_i$	$f_i(x) + \eta_i - \rho_i = b_i$	$\eta_i + \rho_i$

always assigned the top priority or rank (designated typically as P_1). All remaining goals are then ranked, in order of their perceived importance, below the rigid constraint set. Note further that commensurable goals may be (and should be) grouped into a single rank (Ignizio, 1976b; Ignizio, 1982a; Knoll and Englebert, 1978).

Step 3: Given that the solution procedure used in solving LGP models requires a set of simultaneous linear equations (as does LP), all of the goals of (3.14) must be converted into equations through the addition of *logical* variables.

In LP, such logical variables are known as slack and surplus variables (and, when needed, artificial variables). In GP, these logical variables are termed *deviation* variables . . . or goal deviation variables. We summarize this step in Table 3.1.

Having concluded the *first* phase in the conversion of the baseline model into the GP model, we now emphasize that we seek a solution (i.e., **x**) that serves to "minimize" all unwanted deviations. The manner by which we measure the achievement of the minimization of the undesirable goal deviations is what differentiates the various types of GP. Here, we shall use the lexicographic minimum concept—an approach that, as mentioned earlier, will also permit us to consider, as special cases, Archimedean (i.e., minsum) LGP as well as conventional LP. Before proceeding further, let us define the lexicographic minimum, or "lexmin," of an ordered vector.

Lexicographic Minimum: Given an ordered array, say **a**, of nonnegative elements (a_ks), the solution given by $\mathbf{a}^{(1)}$ is preferred to $\mathbf{a}^{(2)}$ if $a_k^{(1)} < a_k^{(2)}$ and all higher order terms (i.e., $a_1, a_2, \ldots, a_{k-1}$) are equal. If no other solution is preferred to **a**, then **a** is the lexicographic minimum.

Thus, if we have two arrays, say $\mathbf{a}^{(r)}$ and $\mathbf{a}^{(s)}$, where

$$\mathbf{a}^{(r)} = (0, 17, 500, 77)^T$$

$$\mathbf{a}^{(s)} = (0, 18, 2, 9)^T$$

then $\mathbf{a}^{(r)}$ is preferred to $\mathbf{a}^{(s)}$.

LGP Conversion Process: Phase Two

We now address the completion of the conversion process, a process that will lead us to the following general form of the lexicographic LGP model:

Find $\mathbf{v}$ so as to

$$\text{lexmin} \quad \mathbf{u}^T = \left\{\mathbf{c}^{(1)T}\mathbf{v}, \ldots, \mathbf{c}^{(k)T}\mathbf{v}, \ldots, \mathbf{c}^{(K)T}\mathbf{v}\right\} \qquad [3.15]$$

s.t.

$$\mathbf{A}\mathbf{v} = \mathbf{b} \qquad [3.16]$$

$$\mathbf{v} \geqslant \mathbf{0} \qquad [3.17]$$

If we observe that

$$\mathbf{v} = \begin{pmatrix} \mathbf{x} \\ \hdashline \boldsymbol{\eta} \\ \hdashline \boldsymbol{\rho} \end{pmatrix} \qquad [3.18]$$

then we may note that (3.16) is simply the representation of all the goals, including their deviation variables (i.e., see Table 3.1) for the problem. It is now left only to explain the meaning and formation of (3.15). The ordered vector $\mathbf{u}^T$, is termed the "achievement" function in GP. Actually, it could be argued that a more appropriate name is the "*un*achievement" function as it really represents a measure of the unachievement encountered in attempting to minimize the rank-ordered set of goal deviations. Thus:

$\mathbf{u}^T$ = the GP achievement function, or vector,

u_k = the kth term of $\mathbf{u}^T$; the term associated with the minimization of all unwanted deviations associated with the set of goals at rank, or priority k, and

$c^{(k)T}$ = the (row vector) of weights associated with the unwanted deviation variables at rank k.

Note in particular the notation used in $\mathbf{c}^{(k)T}$. That is, the "T" superscript simply designates the transpose of the column vector $\mathbf{c}^{(k)}$. The superscript (k) refers, however, to the priority level, or rank, associated with the respective set of weights. For the reader still uncertain as to the procedure, we now describe the conversion via a small numerical example.

An Illustration

In order to both clarify and reinforce the concept of the development of the baseline model, we shall now describe a specific, numerical example. Although far simpler and less complex than would be most real-world problems, the modeling process should still indicate the typical procedure used.

We shall assume that we are concerned with the problems of a specific, high-tech firm. Although this firm produces numerous items, their particular problem is in regard to the manufacture of just two of these products. These products, designated for security as "x_1" and "x_2," are produced in one isolated sector of the plant, via an extremely complex process as carried out on an exceptionally delicate piece of machinery. Once an item is produced, we have *just 24 hours, at the maximum*, to ship and install the item at a remote government installation. That is, unless the finished unit of either product x_1 or x_2 is installed within 24 hours of its manufacture, the product cannot be enhanced chemically and must be scrapped—via an extraordinarily expensive and time-consuming process; a process that would, in fact, drive our company out of business.

The firm has a contract with the government to supply up to 30 units per day of product x_1 and up to 15 units per day of product x_2. However, the government installation, recognizing the delicate nature of the manufacturing process, realizes that receipt of exactly 30 and 15 units of x_1 and x_2, respectively, is unlikely.

The firm makes an estimated profit per unit of \$800 for x_1 and \$1200 for x_2. They state that they certainly wish to maximize their daily profit.

On the single, specially designed processor, it takes just one minute to produce each unit of x_1 and two minutes for each x_2. However, due to the delicate nature of the machine, the firm would like to run it no more than *40 minutes* per every 24-hour period. In the time during which the machine is not running, it may be adjusted and fine tuned so as to satisfy the almost critical manufacturing requirements. Thus, although the machine could conceivably be run for more than 40 minutes per day, this would not be highly desirable to the firm.

To model this problem, in baseline form, we shall first define our structural variables:

x_1 = number of units of product x_1 produced per day;
x_2 = number of units of product x_2 produced per day.

We next form our objectives and goals, as a function of the structural variables.

Our first set of goals will be that of "market demand," the daily (upper) requirements of the government installation. Thus:

$$x_1 \leq 30 \quad \text{(daily demand for } x_1) \qquad [3.19]$$

$$x_2 \leq 15 \quad \text{(daily demand for } x_2) \qquad [3.20]$$

Note carefully that the government, although wanting the upper limits, will accept somewhat fewer units. Further, recall the virtual disaster that would be associated with producing *more* than the daily demands.

The profit objective may be written as follows:

$$\text{maximize } 800x_1 + 1200x_2 \text{ (daily profit)}$$

However, this would be poor modeling practice. That is, in mathematical programming one should always attempt to scale all coefficients so that the difference between the largest and smallest coefficient is minimized. Thus, a more desirable form of the profit objective is

$$\text{maximize } 8x_1 + 12x_2 \quad \text{(daily profit, in \$100 units)} \qquad [3.21]$$

Next, we note that we would like to limit production time per day to 40 minutes total, although the firm does indicate some flexibility about this limit. Thus, we write this goal as

$$x_1 + 2x_2 \leq 40 \quad \text{(daily production time)} \qquad [3.22]$$

Finally, although not explicitly mentioned in our problem description, the firm would obviously like to produce as close to 30 units per day of x_1 and 15 units per day of x_2. In doing so, they not only increase their profits but also keep the customer happy. We shall wait for a moment before actually formulating these last goals. However, note that they are associated with (3.19) and (3.20).

Our next step is to convert any objectives into goals. The only objective listed in (3.19)-(3.22) is that of maximizing profit. Assuming that the firm's aspired daily profit from these two products is $100,000, we convert

$$\text{maximize} \quad 8x_1 + 12x_2$$

into

$$8x_1 + 12x_2 \geq 1000 \qquad [3.23]$$

We are now ready to rank order all goals, in conjunction with discussions with the firm's decision makers. For purpose of discussion, we shall assume that the order of presentation coincides with the order of preference. Further, it is obvious that the first two goals (daily requirements) are the only ones that are rigid in this problem. Thus, letting P_k refer to the kth priority or rank:

P_1: produce no more items per day of each item than demanded.

P_2: achieve a profit of $100,000 per day, or more.

P_3: attempt to keep processing time to 40 minutes or less per day.

P_4: attempt to supply as close to 30 units and 15 units of x_1 and x_2, respectively, per day. Further, we shall assume that the firm considers supply x_2 to be one and a half times more important than x_1.

After including the necessary goal deviation variables (i.e., n_i and ρ_i) and forming the achievement function, we develop the final form of the lexicographic LGP model as shown below:

$$\text{lexmin } \mathbf{u}^T = \{(\rho_1 + \rho_2), (\eta_3), (\rho_4), (\eta_1 + 1.5\eta_2)\} \qquad [3.24]$$

s.t.

$$x_1 \qquad + \eta_1 - \rho_1 = 30$$

$$x_2 + \eta_2 - \rho_2 = 15$$

$$8x_1 + 12x_2 + \eta_3 - \rho_3 = 1000 \qquad [3.25]$$

$$x_1 + \ 2x_x + \eta_4 - \rho_4 = 40$$

$$\mathbf{x},\ \boldsymbol{\eta},\ \boldsymbol{\rho} \geqslant \mathbf{0} \qquad [3.26]$$

Notice, in particular, that two (or more) goals may be combined in one priority level *if they are commensurable* (i.e., credible weights may be assigned to each goal so that they may be expressed in a single performance measure). This occurs in P_4 (the fourth term of $\mathbf{u}^T$). Further, *all rigid constraints* are *always combined* in P_1, even if not in the same units, as they *must* be achieved if the program is to be implementable.

The model of (3.24)-(3.26) may be rewritten, in a more general form, as

$$\text{lexmin } \mathbf{u}^T = \left\{ \mathbf{c}^{(1)T}\mathbf{v},\ \mathbf{c}^{(2)T}\mathbf{v},\ \mathbf{c}^{(3)T}\mathbf{v},\ \mathbf{c}^{(4)T}\mathbf{v} \right\}$$

s.t.

$$\mathbf{A}\mathbf{v} = \mathbf{b}$$

$$\mathbf{v} \geqslant \mathbf{0}$$

where

$$\mathbf{v}^T = (x_1\ x_2 \ :\ \eta_1\ \eta_2\ \eta_3\ \eta_4\ :\ \rho_1\ \rho_2\ \rho_3\ \rho_4)$$

$$\mathbf{c}^{(1)T} = (0\ \ 0\ \ :\ 0\ \ 0\ \ 0\ \ 0\ \ :\ 1\ \ 1\ \ 0\ \ 0\ )$$

$$\mathbf{c}^{(2)T} = (0\ \ 0\ \ :\ 0\ \ 0\ \ 1\ \ 0\ \ :\ 0\ \ 0\ \ 0\ \ 0\ )$$

$$\mathbf{c}^{(3)T} = (0\ \ 0\ \ :\ 0\ \ 0\ \ 0\ \ 0\ \ :\ 0\ \ 0\ \ 0\ \ 1\ )$$

$$\mathbf{c}^{(4)T} = (0\ \ 0\ \ :\ 1\ \ 1.5\ \ 0\ \ 0\ \ :\ 0\ \ 0\ \ 0\ \ 0\ )$$

$$\mathbf{A} = \begin{pmatrix} 1 & 0 & : & 1 & 0 & 0 & 0 & : & -1 & 0 & 0 & 0 \\ 0 & 1 & : & 0 & 1 & 0 & 0 & : & 0 & -1 & 0 & 0 \\ 8 & 12 & : & 0 & 0 & 1 & 0 & : & 0 & 0 & -1 & 0 \\ 1 & 2 & : & 0 & 0 & 0 & 1 & : & 0 & 0 & 0 & -1 \end{pmatrix}$$

$$\mathbf{b}^T = (30 \quad 15 \quad 1000 \quad 40)$$

As we shall see in Chapter 5, the optimal solution to this model is

$$\mathbf{v}^* = (30 \quad 15 \quad : \quad 0 \quad 0 \quad 580 \quad 0 \quad : \quad 0 \quad 0 \quad 0 \quad 20)^T$$

$$\mathbf{u}^* = (0 \quad 580 \quad 20 \quad 0)^T$$

From **v***, we note that $x_1^* = 30$ and $x_2^* = 15$ and thus we produce exactly the daily limits. Observing **u***, we can determine how well our goals were met.

- $u_1^* = 0$; thus all rigid constraints are satisfied.
- $u_2^* = 580$; the result is 580 units *below* the goal of 1000. Thus, we achieve a daily profit of $42,000 rather than $100,000.
- $u_3^* = 20$; the result is 20 units *over* the aspired goal of 40. Consequently, our machine must be run for 60 minutes per day rather than 40.
- $u_4^* = 0$; the last set of goals are completely satisfied.

Good and Poor Modeling Practices

Note the achievement function of (3.24), or the general form of (3.15). This function is an *ordered vector*, with each element corresponding to the measure of the minimization of certain *unwanted* goal deviations. When one refers back to the earlier definition of the lexicographic minimum, we note that this definition is, in fact, based upon the notion of an ordered vector. Despite this, some employ a GP achievement function (which they typically term as an "objective function") that indicates a *summation* of the individual elements of $\mathbf{u}^T$. That is, they will write $\mathbf{u}^T$ in (3.24) as follows:

$$\text{minimize} \quad P_1(\rho_1 + \rho_2) + P_2(\eta_3) + P_3(\rho_4) + P_4(\eta_1 + 1.5\eta_2)$$

where P_k indicates the rank, or priority, of the term in parentheses. Although in common use, this notation is exceptionally poor practice as it totally contradicts the very definition of the lexicographic minimum (or of "preemptive priorities"). The real problem appears, however, when those using such notation attempt to develop any extensions of GP or supporting proofs. That is, the invalid summations serve to, quite often, totally confuse those pursuing such extensions. Consequently, it is my belief that, despite the "tradition" of such a form, it is mathematical nonsense and should be avoided.

Another modeling practice sometimes advocated by others is to construct goals *without the inclusion of any structural variables.* To illustrate this, consider the following example;

$$(G_1) \quad x_1 + x_2 + \eta_1 - \enclose{circle}{\rho_1} = 40$$

$$(G_2) \quad \eta_1 + \eta_2 - \enclose{circle}{\rho_2} = 10$$

Here, the circled deviation variables are those we wish to minimize. Thus, G_1 is $x_1 + x_2 \leq 40$ wherein G_2 is an attempt to state that in G_1 the negative deviation from 40 should be 10 units or less. I claim that the following representation is more effective:

$$(G_1') \quad x_1 + x_2 + \eta_1 - \enclose{circle}{\rho_1} = 40$$

$$(G_2') \quad x_1 + x_2 + \enclose{circle}{\eta_2} - \rho_2 = 30$$

The reader should note that both representations are equivalent. However, the first representation will require, when solved by any LGP algorithm, *more variables* than the second. The reason for this will become clear in Chapter 4. Here, we simply note that the so-called initial basic feasible solution in LGP always consists of the negative deviation variables (n_is). As such, *each* η_i must appear in *exactly one goal.* Such is not the case in G_1 and G_2. Consequently, to alleviate this, *at least* one new variable must be added to the formulation. Thus, although G_1 and G_2 mean the same thing as G_1' and G_2', the latter is a more computationally efficient representation. To conclude, we simply note that it is *never* good practice to form a goal consisting solely of deviation variables—and an alternate, proper representation may always be found.

We also note that the rigid constraints should always appear, *separately*, in priority level one (i.e., as u_1). All remaining goals should be ranked below them but *may* appear in a single priority level (or as grouped sets) *if* reasonable weights may be found so as to achieve commensurability. Further, we should always realize the implication of separate priority levels. That is, the achievement of P_r always preempts that of P_s if $s > r$ and thus the goals at P_s can be achieved only to the point that they do not degrade any higher-order goals. It is for this reason that it is poor practice to have more than about 5 or 6 priority levels. That is, the likelihood of being able to deal with any goals at a priority level of, say, ten is virtually nil.

A *good* GP model will make good sense. That is, it should be logical and express the problem accurately. If it does not, one should seek to improve the model so that it does make sense. Some checks that should always be made include:

(1) Are all the rigid constraints (and *only* the rigid constraints) at priority one?
(2) Are the *unwanted* deviations those that appear in the achievement function?
(3) Are there more than 5 or 6 priority levels (real-world problems *typically* have no more than 2 to 5 priority levels)?
(4) Are all sets of commensurable goals grouped within the same priority level?
(5) Do any goals consist solely of deviation variables? If so, replace them as discussed earlier.

4. AN ALGORITHM FOR SOLUTION

As discussed in Chapter 2, a number of different algorithms (and associated computer software) have been developed for the solution of the lexicographic LGP model. Further, the best of these algorithms (e.g., MULTIPLEX; Ignizio, 1983e, 1985a, forthcoming) are capable of solving models of comparable sizes (i.e., several thousands of rows by tens of thousands of variables) and with equivalent computational efficiency as that found in commercial simplex software (i.e., for conventional LP models; Ignizio, 1983e, 1984, 1985a, forthcoming).

In this chapter we shall address just one version of the many LGP algorithms, a version using multiphase simplex. For those with a familiarity with LP, we note that multiphase simplex is simply a straightforward and rather transparent extension of the well-known "two phase" simplex procedure (Charnes and Cooper, 1961; Ignizio, 1982a; Lasdon, 1970; Murtagh, 1981) for conventional LP.

The Transformed Model

In Chapter 3, we presented the general form of the lexicographic LGP model in (3.15)-(3.18). We have rewritten this model below:

Find **v** so as to

$$\text{lexmin } \mathbf{u}^T = \left\{ \mathbf{c}^{(1)T}\mathbf{v}, \ldots, \mathbf{c}^{(k)T}\mathbf{v}, \ldots, \mathbf{c}^{(K)T}\mathbf{v} \right\} \qquad [4.1]$$

s.t.

$$\mathbf{A}\mathbf{v} = \mathbf{b} \qquad [4.2]$$

$$\mathbf{v} \geqslant \mathbf{0} \qquad [4.3]$$

where

$$\mathbf{v} = \begin{pmatrix} \mathbf{x} \\ --- \\ \boldsymbol{\eta} \\ --- \\ \boldsymbol{\rho} \end{pmatrix} \qquad [4.4]$$

Note that $\boldsymbol{\eta}$ and $\boldsymbol{\rho}$ are the logical (or goal deviation) variables whereas **x** is the structural variable.

Further, as $c_j^{(k)}$ represents the weight given to variable j, at priority or rank k, then all $c_j^{(k)}$ are, *in LGP*, nonnegative. That is,

$$\mathbf{c}^{(k)T} \geq \mathbf{0} \qquad \forall k \qquad [4.5]$$

Although the previous model represents and conveniently summarizes the lexicographic LGP model, we shall work with a transformation of this model. This "transformed model" is also known as the "tabular" model or "reduced form" model. The advantages of the transformed model include the fact that, from it, various LGP conditions may be easily derived. We now proceed with the development of the transformed LGP model.

We first note that the set of goals is given as:

$$\mathbf{A}\mathbf{v} = \mathbf{b} \qquad [4.6]$$

However, the mxn matrix, **A**, may be partitioned into:

$$\mathbf{A} = (\mathbf{B}:\mathbf{N})$$

where:

$\mathbf{B}$ = a mxm nonsingular matrix, designated as the *basis* matrix, and
$\mathbf{N}$ = a mx(n – m) matrix

Further, the variable set, **v**, may be similarly partitioned into:

$$\mathbf{v} = \begin{pmatrix} \mathbf{v}_B \\ \text{----} \\ \mathbf{v}_N \end{pmatrix} \quad [4.7]$$

where:

$\mathbf{v}_B$ = the set of *basic variables*—those associated with **B** and
$\mathbf{v}_N$ = the set of *nonbasic variables*—those associated with **N**

Consequently, we may rewrite (4.6) as

$$\mathbf{B}\mathbf{v}_B + \mathbf{N}\mathbf{v}_N = \mathbf{b} \quad [4.8]$$

and, as **B** is nonsingular (and thus has an inverse), we may premultiply each term in (4.8) by $\mathbf{B}^{-1}$ to obtain

$$\mathbf{B}^{-1}\mathbf{B}\mathbf{v}_B + \mathbf{B}^{-1}\mathbf{N}\mathbf{v}_N = \mathbf{B}^{-1}\mathbf{b}$$

or

$$\mathbf{v}_B + \mathbf{B}^{-1}\mathbf{N}\mathbf{v}_N = \mathbf{B}^{-1}\mathbf{b}$$

and, solving for $\mathbf{v}_B$:

$$\mathbf{v}_B = \mathbf{B}^{-1}\mathbf{b} - \mathbf{B}^{-1}\mathbf{N}\mathbf{v}_N \quad [4.9]$$

Next, examine the LGP achievement function as given in (4.1). The general, or k^{th} element of **u** is given as

$$\mathbf{c}^{(k)T}\mathbf{v}$$

However, recall that **v** was partitioned according to (4.7) and thus the above term may be rewritten as

$$\mathbf{c}_B^{(k)T}\mathbf{v}_B + \mathbf{c}_N^{(k)T}\mathbf{v}_N \quad [4.10]$$

wherein the subscripts for $\mathbf{c}$ reflect those coefficients associated with the set of basic variables or those associated with the nonbasic variables—"B" or "N," respectively.

We may now, using (4.9), substitute for $\mathbf{v}_B$ in (4.10) to obtain

$$\mathbf{c}^{(k)T}\mathbf{v} = \mathbf{c}_B^{(k)T}\mathbf{B}^{-1}\mathbf{b} - (\mathbf{c}_B^{(k)T}\mathbf{B}^{-1}\mathbf{N} - \mathbf{c}_N^{(k)T})\mathbf{v}_N \qquad [4.11]$$

Further, let

$$\beta = \mathbf{B}^{-1}\mathbf{b} \qquad [4.12]$$

$$\pi^{(k)T} = \mathbf{c}_B^{(k)T}\mathbf{B}^{-1} \qquad [4.13]$$

$$\alpha = \mathbf{B}^{-1}\mathbf{N} \quad \text{and} \quad \alpha_j = \mathbf{B}^{-1}\mathbf{a}_j \qquad [4.14]$$

where $\mathbf{a}_j$ is the jth column of $\mathbf{A}$.

Using the above, we may write the general form of the LGP model from (4.1)-(4.3) in the "transformed" or "reduced" form as given below.

Find $\mathbf{v}$ so as to

$$\text{lexmin } \mathbf{u}^T = \{[\mathbf{c}_B^{(1)T}\beta - (\pi^{(1)T}\mathbf{N} - \mathbf{c}_N^{(1)T})\mathbf{v}_N], \ldots,$$

$$[\mathbf{c}_B^{(K)T}\beta - (\pi^{(K)T}\mathbf{N} - \mathbf{c}_N^{(K)T})\mathbf{v}_N]\} \qquad [4.15]$$

s.t.

$$\mathbf{v}_B = \beta - \mathbf{B}^{-1}\mathbf{N}\mathbf{v}_N \qquad [4.16]$$

$$\mathbf{v} = \begin{pmatrix} \mathbf{v}_B \\ \text{----} \\ \mathbf{v}_N \end{pmatrix} \geqslant \mathbf{0} \qquad [4.17]$$

An alternative and quite convenient way in which we may summarize (4.15)-(4.17) is by means of a tableau, as shown in Table 4.1.

Basic Feasible Solution

We may define a *basic solution* as one in which all nonbasic variables are set at their bound. For our purposes, this bound shall be zero. Thus,

TABLE 4.1
LGP Tableau

	v_B	v_N	β (or rhs)
v_B	$B^{-1}B = I$	$B^{-1}N$	$B^{-1}b$
P_1		$c_B^{(1)T}B^{-1}N - c_N^{(1)T}$	$c_B^{(1)T}B^{-1}b$
·	0	·	·
P_K		$c_B^{(K)T}B^{-1}N - c_N^{(K)T}$	$c_B^{(K)T}B^{-1}b$

if $\mathbf{v}_N = \mathbf{0}$, a basic solution results. More specifically, if $\mathbf{v}_N = \mathbf{0}$, then $\mathbf{B}^{-1}\mathbf{N}\mathbf{v}_N = \mathbf{0}$ and thus

$$\mathbf{v}_B = \mathbf{B}^{-1}\mathbf{b} - \mathbf{B}^{-1}\mathbf{N}\mathbf{v}_N = \mathbf{B}^{-1}\mathbf{b} \qquad [4.18]$$

Further, a *basic feasible solution* is one wherein all terms in (4.18) are nonnegative. Thus, a basic feasible solution is:

$$\mathbf{v} = \begin{bmatrix} \mathbf{v}_B \geqslant \mathbf{0} \\ \text{-------} \\ \mathbf{v}_N = \mathbf{0} \end{bmatrix} \geqslant \mathbf{0} \qquad [4.19]$$

In LGP, as in LP, the optimal solution may always be found as a basic feasible solution (Charnes and Cooper, 1961).

Associated Conditions

The three primary conditions associated with the reduced form of the LGP model are *feasibility, implementability,* and *optimality*. Given that $\mathbf{v}_N = \mathbf{0}$, these terms are defined as follows:

Feasibility: If $\boldsymbol{\beta} = \mathbf{B}^{-1}\mathbf{b} \geq \mathbf{0}$, the resultant solution, or program, is denoted as being feasible.

Implementability: If $\mathbf{c}_B^{(1)T}\boldsymbol{\beta} = \mathbf{c}_B^{(1)T}\mathbf{B}^{-1}\mathbf{b} = 0$, then the resultant program ($\mathbf{v}_B$) is designated as being an *implementable* solution. That is, the top ranked set of goals (i.e., the set of rigid constraints) are all satisfied.

Now, before defining the conditions for the optimality of a given program for an LGP model, let us first note that, in (4.15), the terms

$$\pi^{(k)T}\mathbf{N} - \mathbf{c}_N^{(k)T} \quad [4.20]$$

are designated as the vector of *increased costs* as this indicates just how much the kth term of the achievement function will increase as $\mathbf{v}_N$ changes.

We shall let the jth element of (4.20) be designated as

$$d_j^{(k)} = z_j^{(k)} - c_j^{(k)} \quad [4.21]$$

wherein

$$z_j^{(k)} = (\pi^{(k)T}\mathbf{N})_j = \pi^{(k)T}\mathbf{a}_j \quad [4.22]$$

Consequently, associated with each nonbasic variable is a *column vector* of $d_j^{(k)}$ elements. This vector is termed, in LGP, as the vector of multidimensional shadow prices or as simply the *shadow price vector*, $\mathbf{d}_j$.

Optimality: If every shadow price vector, $\mathbf{d}_j$, is *lexicographically nonpositive*, the associated basic feasible solution ($\mathbf{v}_B$) is optimal for the given LGP model. This optimal program is designated as $\mathbf{v}_B^*$.

A lexicographically nonpositive vector is one, in turn, in which the first nonzero element is negative. Of course, a vector of solely zeros is also lexicographically nonpositive.

We may note that "implementability" is a condition that is unique to GP. Further, unlike LP, *there is no condition of unboundedness in GP.* This may be observed by simply examining the achievement function form given originally in (4.1), and repeated below:

$$\text{lexmin } \mathbf{u}^T = \{\mathbf{c}^{(1)T}\mathbf{v}, \ldots, \mathbf{c}^{(K)T}\mathbf{v}\}$$

Now, $\mathbf{u}^T$ could only be unbounded (in the case of seeking the lexicographic minimum of $\mathbf{u}^T$) if one or more elements of $\mathbf{u}^T$ could decrease to minus infinity. This is obviously impossible because

$$\mathbf{v} \geq \mathbf{0} \quad \textit{and} \quad \mathbf{c}^{(k)} \geq \mathbf{0} \quad \text{for all k}$$

Thus, the absolute minimum value for any u_k is zero.[7] Despite this, other material or texts on GP sometimes discuss the unbounded condition for LGP as if it were actually possible and, in fact, even propose checks within their proposed algorithms for solutions. The implementation of such unnecessary checks simply increases computation time. Evidently, those proposing such conditions and checks are simply copying, without thought to the rationale, the checks for unboundedness that exist in LP. This situation, as well as numerous others, provides ample reason to not blindly treat GP, or LGP, as simply "an extension of LP." In fact, a more logical view would be to consider LP as but a special subclass of LGP.

Algorithm for Solution: A Narrative Description

Before proceeding to a listing of the specific steps of our algorithm for solution of the LGP model, let us first attempt to describe the overall nature of this algorithm. As with any algorithm for mathematical programming, our assumption is that a correct mathematical model has been developed.

Initially, we focus our attention on priority level one, the achievement of the complete set of rigid constraints. Thus, our initial motivation is to develop a basic solution that (if possible) simultaneously satisfies all the rigid constraints. This is accomplished whenever $a_1 = 0$. In our attempt to achieve this, we initially set all structural variables and positive deviation variables nonbasic. Consequently, our first basis consists solely of the set of negative deviation variables. Typically, this basis (which, in essence, is the "do nothing" solution) will not satisfy all rigid constraints and thus we initiate the simplex pivoting procedure. Specifically, we exchange one basic variable for one nonbasic variable *if* such an exchange will: (a) retain feasibility, and (b) lead to an improved solution—one that more closely satisfies the set of rigid constraints. The pivoting step is then repeated until all rigid constraints are satisfied as closely as is possible (i.e., until a_1 reaches its minimum value—a value of zero, it is hoped).

Having obtained the minimum value for a_1, we next attempt to minimize a_2 without degrading the value previously obtained for our higher priority level (i.e., a_1). Minimization of a_2 is accomplished, once again, via the simplex pivoting process. However, in addition to considering the feasibility and improvement of any proposed exchange, we must also not permit an exchange that would degrade the value of a_1 (i.e., increase its value).

The procedure continues in this manner until the lexicographic minimum of **a** is finally obtained. Those readers with a previous exposure to conventional linear programming will recognize that the procedure used is but a slightly modified version of the well-known simplex algorithm; specifically the two-phase simplex procedure used in most commercial simplex software packages.

The Revised Multiphase Simplex Algorithm

The algorithm for the solution of the LGP model, as is described next, is termed the revised multiphase simplex algorithm. As such, it is basically a straightforward modification of revised simplex for LP wherein the so-called two-phase simplex process is utilized. The modification itself permits *multiple* "phases," rather than just two as in conventional LP.

Under the assumption that the algorithm is to be ultimately implemented via a computer, the information maintained in computer storage must consist of some representation of the original LGP model as given in (4.1)-(4.3). Specifically, we store **A**, **b**, and $\mathbf{c}^{(k)T}$ for all k.

We begin the algorithm by assuming that we have an initial basic feasible solution, some representation of $\mathbf{B}^{-1}$ and the associated program: $\boldsymbol{\beta} = \mathbf{B}^{-1}\mathbf{b}$ (with the latter designated as the "current right-hand side"). When employing the LGP model, these are trivial requirements because, *initially*, $\boldsymbol{\eta} = \mathbf{b}$ and $\mathbf{x}, \boldsymbol{\rho} = \mathbf{0}$ will always provide a basic feasible solution (we assume that all goals are written with nonnegative right-hand sides). Further, the basis associated with $\mathbf{v}_B = \boldsymbol{\eta}$ is the identity matrix, **I**, and thus $\mathbf{B}^{-1} = \mathbf{I}$ initially.

We may then generate the multidimensional shadow price vectors, $\mathbf{d}_j$, for all nonbasic variables and determine whether or not the present basic feasible solution is optimal.[8] If so, we may stop. Otherwise, we must proceed to a *pivoting* operation. Pivoting involves the exchange of a nonbasic variable for a basic variable in a manner such that:

(1) the new solution is still a basic feasible solution, and
(2) the resultant value of $\mathbf{u}^T$ is improved, or is at least no worse than before the pivot.

Once we have pivoted, we simply update B^{-1} and $\boldsymbol{\beta}$ and repeat the process. In actual practice, we may augment the procedure described above by numerous refinements and shortcuts so as to substantially improve computational performance. We now list the steps of the revised simplex procedure for LGP.

Step 1. Initialization. Let $\mathbf{v}_B = \boldsymbol{\eta}$. Thus, $\mathbf{B} = \mathbf{I}$, $\mathbf{B}^{-1} = \mathbf{I}$ and $\boldsymbol{\beta} = \mathbf{b}$. Set k = 1. Initially, all variables are unchecked.

Step 2. Develop the pricing vector. Determine:

$$\boldsymbol{\pi}^{(k)T} = \mathbf{c}_B^{(k)T}\mathbf{B}^{-1} \qquad [4.23]$$

Step 3. Price out all UNCHECKED, nonbasic columns. Compute:

$$d_j^{(k)} = \boldsymbol{\pi}^{(k)T}\mathbf{a}_j - c_j^{(k)} \qquad [4.24]$$

$$\text{for all } j \in \hat{N}$$

where $\hat{N}$ is the set of nonbasic *and* unchecked variables.

Step 4. Selection of entering nonbasic variables. Examine those $d_j^{(k)}$ as computed in step 3. If none are positive, proceed to step 8. Otherwise, select the nonbasic variable with the most positive $d_j^{(k)}$ (ties may be broken arbitrarily) as the entering variable. Designate this variable as v_q.

Step 5. Update the entering column. Evaluate:

$$\boldsymbol{\alpha}_q = \mathbf{B}^{-1}\mathbf{a}_q \qquad [4.25]$$

Step 6. Determine the leaving basic variable. We shall designate the leaving variable row as i = p. Using the present representation of $\boldsymbol{\beta}$ and the values of $\boldsymbol{\alpha}_q$, as derived in step 5, we determine:

$$\frac{\beta_p}{\alpha_{p,q}} = \min_i \left\{ \frac{\beta_i}{\alpha_{i,q}} \right\} \text{ for } \alpha_{i,q} > 0 \qquad [4.26]$$

Again, ties may be broken arbitrarily. The basic variable associated with row i = p is the leaving variable, $v_{B,p}$.

Step 7. Pivot.[9] We replace $\mathbf{a}_p$ in $\mathbf{B}$ by $\mathbf{a}_q$ and compute the *new* basis inverse, $\mathbf{B}^{-1}$. Return to step 2.

Step 8. Convergence check. If either one (or both) of the following conditions holds, STOP as we have found the optimal solution:

(a) if all $d_j^{(k)}$ as computed in step 3 are negative, or

(b) if $k = \mathbf{K}$ (where $\mathbf{K}$ = number of priority levels, or terms in $\mathbf{u}^T$). Otherwise, "check" all nonbasic variables associated with a negative $d_j^{(k)}$, set $k = k + 1$ and return to step 2.

The above eight steps represent the primary elements of the revised multiphase simplex algorithm for LGP. However, it must be realized that truly efficient computer software for the implementation of such an algorithm will typically involve numerous modifications and refinements tailored about the specific advantages as well as limitations of the digital computer.

In the following chapter, we illustrate the implementation of the described algorithm on a numerical example. However, before proceeding to that discussion, we next examine, in more detail, certain steps of the above algorithm.

The Pivoting Procedure in LGP

The heart of the solution algorithm for the LGP model is a procedure denoted as pivoting. In essence, pivoting involves the modification of a prior basic feasible solution. Associated with every basic feasible solution, $\mathbf{v}_B$, is a basis, $\mathbf{B}$. This basis is composed of a set of m linearly independent column vectors from $\mathbf{A}$, the matrix of "technological coefficients" that appears in the statement of the LGP goals (i.e., $\mathbf{Av} = \mathbf{b}$).

In its most elementary form, pivoting involves the exchange of a column vector of $\mathbf{B}$ (as associated with a present basic variable) for a nonbasic column vector from $\mathbf{N}$. That is, a nonbasic variable is said to "enter" the basis while a basic variable "leaves" the basis. Such an exchange is made if it results in an improvement in the lexicographic minimum of $\mathbf{u}^T$; or, at worst, if $\mathbf{u}^T$ is not degraded.

The choice of the nonbasic vector to enter the basis is made via an operation termed the "price out" procedure. Simply put, the price out procedure evaluates the *potential* improvement in $\mathbf{u}^T$ for each candidate nonbasic variable—and selects the one that *appears* to provide the greatest reduction. The determination of the basic variable that is to leave the basis is slightly more involved. Given that a new variable (i.e., a presently nonbasic variable) is to enter the basis, a basic variable must obviously leave—and the choice of the basic variable that departs is not arbitrary. Specifically, the choice is made so that the new basis is associated with a new basic *feasible* solution. This may be illustrated as follows. First, observe the transformed form of the LGP model that reflects the basic feasible solution, for example:

$$\mathbf{v}_B = \mathbf{B}^{-1}\mathbf{b} - \mathbf{B}^{-1}\mathbf{N}\mathbf{v}_N$$

with $\boldsymbol{\beta} = \mathbf{B}^{-1}\mathbf{b}$ and realizing that only a single nonbasic variable is to enter the basis, we may rewrite the above expression as

$$\mathbf{v}_B = \boldsymbol{\beta} - \mathbf{B}^{-1}\mathbf{a}_q \, v_q$$

where q is the subscript associated with the entering nonbasic variable. However, we may replace $\mathbf{B}^{-1}\mathbf{a}_q$ with α_q. Thus,

$$\mathbf{v}_B = \boldsymbol{\beta} - \boldsymbol{\alpha}_q \, v_q$$

Rewriting $\mathbf{v}_B$ in terms of each of its components, we have

$$\begin{pmatrix} v_{B,1} \\ v_{B,2} \\ \vdots \\ v_{B,m} \end{pmatrix} = \begin{pmatrix} \beta_1 \\ \beta_2 \\ \vdots \\ \beta_m \end{pmatrix} - \begin{pmatrix} \alpha_{1,q} \\ \alpha_{2,q} \\ \vdots \\ \alpha_{m,q} \end{pmatrix} v_q$$

Thus, as v_q increases, β_i decreases *if* $\alpha_{i,q}$ is positive. That is,

$$\hat{\beta}_i = \beta_i - \alpha_{i,q} v_q$$

where $\hat{\beta}_i$ is the new value of β_i. In order that $\mathbf{v}_B$ remain feasible, each β_i must remain nonnegative. As such, if any $\alpha_{i,q}$ is positive, the corresponding value of β_i will decrease, eventually passing through zero. Thus, the first such β_i that would reach zero determines the so-called blocking basic variable—the basic variable that must leave the basis if v_q enters. This leads directly to the departing basic variable rule given as (4.26) in the previous algorithm.

The operation of the pivoting procedure, summarized so briefly in step 7 of the algorithm, is to compute the new inverse as a result of the pivot. Nearly all present day commercial software for the conventional simplex method (i.e., for LP) or that for LGP utilize the so-called product form of the inverse (Charnes and Cooper, 1961; Ignizio, 1982a; Lasdon, 1970; Murtagh, 1981) to accomplish this evaluation. There are, however, several alternate approaches and, in fact, we shall present one of these in the chapter to follow (in the discussion of the tabular simplex process for LGP). This method is termed the "explicit form of the inverse" and it, as well as its variations, provides a reasonably computationally efficient approach to LGP, whether performed by hand or on the computer.

5. ALGORITHM ILLUSTRATION

To illustrate the implementation of the algorithm as listed in Chapter 4, we apply that procedure to the same LGP model originally formed in Chapter 3 and given in (3.24)-(3.26). Specifically, the problem addressed is as follows:

Find **x** so as to

$$\text{lexmin } \mathbf{u}^T = \{(\rho_1 + \rho_2), (\eta_3), (\rho_4), (\eta_1 + 1.5\eta_2)\} \qquad [5.1]$$

s.t.

$$\left.\begin{aligned} x_1 + \qquad + \eta_1 - \rho_1 &= 30 \\ x_2 + \eta_2 - \rho_2 &= 15 \\ 8x_1 + 12x_2 + \eta_3 - \rho_3 &= 1000 \\ x_1 + 2x_2 + \eta_4 - \rho_4 &= 40 \end{aligned}\right\} \qquad [5.2]$$

$$\mathbf{x}, \eta, \rho \geqslant \mathbf{0} \qquad [5.3]$$

However, the above form of the model is not convenient to work with and thus we replace it by the more general form:

Find **v** so as to

$$\text{lexmin } \mathbf{u}^T = \{\mathbf{c}^{(1)T}\mathbf{v}, \mathbf{c}^{(2)T}\mathbf{v}, \mathbf{c}^{(3)T}\mathbf{v}, \mathbf{c}^{(4)T}\mathbf{v}\} \qquad [5.4]$$

s.t.

$$\mathbf{Av} = \mathbf{b} \qquad [5.5]$$

$$\mathbf{v} \geqslant \mathbf{0} \qquad [5.6]$$

where

$$\mathbf{v}^T = (x_1\ x_2 : \eta_1\ \eta_2\ \eta_3\ \eta_4 : \rho_1\ \rho_2\ \rho_3\ \rho_4)$$

or

$$\mathbf{v}^T = (v_1\ v_2 : v_3\ v_4\ v_5\ v_6 : v_7\ v_8\ v_9\ v_{10})$$

and

$$c^{(1)T} = (0 \quad 0 \quad : \quad 0 \quad 0 \quad 0 \quad 0 \quad : \quad 1 \quad 1 \quad 0 \quad 0)$$
$$c^{(2)T} = (0 \quad 0 \quad : \quad 0 \quad 0 \quad 1 \quad 0 \quad : \quad 0 \quad 0 \quad 0 \quad 0)$$
$$c^{(3)T} = (0 \quad 0 \quad : \quad 0 \quad 0 \quad 0 \quad 0 \quad : \quad 0 \quad 0 \quad 0 \quad 1)$$
$$c^{(4)T} = (0 \quad 0 \quad : \quad 1 \quad 1.5 \quad 0 \quad 0 \quad : \quad 0 \quad 0 \quad 0 \quad 0)$$

$$\mathbf{A} = \begin{pmatrix} 1 & 0 & : & 1 & 0 & 0 & 0 & : & -1 & 0 & 0 & 0 \\ 0 & 1 & : & 0 & 1 & 0 & 0 & : & 0 & -1 & 0 & 0 \\ 8 & 12 & : & 0 & 0 & 1 & 0 & : & 0 & 0 & -1 & 0 \\ 1 & 2 & : & 0 & 0 & 0 & 1 & : & 0 & 0 & 0 & -1 \end{pmatrix}$$

$$\mathbf{b} = \begin{pmatrix} 30 \\ 15 \\ 1000 \\ 40 \end{pmatrix}$$

The Tableau

In Chapter 4, Table 4.1, we presented one particular form of the LGP tableau. Specifically, that version is termed the "full" or "extended" tableau form. Actually, we might term it the "too full" tableau as it contains far more information than is actually needed to perform the algorithm. Although the full tableau is often used in textbook presentations, it is simply not suitable for realistic computer implementation. Thus, here we use an alternative and considerably more convenient tableau form. We advocate the use of this tableau whether one is solving the problem by hand or developing a computer program for reasonably efficient solution. This tableau is shown in Table 5.1.

Note that this tableau contains

$\mathbf{B}^{-1}$ the inverse of the present basis;

$\boldsymbol{\beta}$ the present right-hand side ($\mathbf{v}_B = \mathbf{B}^{-1}\mathbf{b}$), or program;

$\mathbf{u}$ the achievement vector;

and Π the matrix of $\pi_j^{(k)}$ elements.

TABLE 5.1
LGP Tableau, Explicit Form of Inverse

$v_{B,1}$ ⋮ $v_{B,i}$ ⋮ $v_{B,m}$	B^{-1}	β
$\pi^{(1)T}$ ⋮ $\pi^{(K)T}$	Π	**u**

Remarking on Π, we note that each row in Π, given as $\pi^{(k)T}$ in general, is the pricing vector as specified in step 2 of the algorithm of Chapter 4.

Actually, the section of this tableau that contains **u** is not really needed in performing the algorithm. We keep it merely to note the continuing improvement of **u** in each iteration.

We may now write the associated *initial* tableau for the problem given in (5.4)-(5.6).

v_3	1	0	0	0	30	$\beta = B^{-1}b$
v_4	0	1	0	0	15	
v_5	0	0	1	0	1000	
v_6	0	0	0	1	40	
$\pi^{(1)T}$	0	0	0	0	0	**u**
$\pi^{(2)T}$	0	0	1	0	1000	
$\pi^{(3)T}$	0	0	0	0	0	
$\pi^{(4)T}$	1	1.5	0	0	52.5	

Note carefully that v_3 through v_6 (which correspond to η_1 through η_4) are the initial set of basic variables, as specified in step 1 of the algorithm. That is,

$$v_{B,1} = v_3 = \eta_1$$

$$v_{B,2} = v_4 = \eta_2$$

$$v_{B,3} = v_5 = \eta_3$$

$$v_{B,4} = v_6 = \eta_4$$

Further, the $\boldsymbol{\alpha}_j$'s corresponding to this set of variables form the columns of the basis inverse—for the intial basis *as well as for any other basic feasible solution.*

Because the initial basis is equal to **I**, the associated right-hand side (rhs), or $\boldsymbol{\beta}$, is

$$\boldsymbol{\beta} = \mathbf{B}^{-1}\,\mathbf{b} = \mathbf{I}\,\mathbf{b} = \begin{pmatrix} 30 \\ 15 \\ 1000 \\ 40 \end{pmatrix}$$

Each element of Π is then given by (4.23), that is,

$$\pi^{(k)T} = \mathbf{c}_B^{(k)T}\,\mathbf{B}^{-1}$$

To the right of the Π matrix are the achievement vector values as given by (4.15). Specifically,

$$u_k = \mathbf{c}_B^{(k)T}\,\mathbf{B}^{-1}\,\mathbf{b} = \pi^{(k)T}\,\mathbf{B} \qquad \forall k$$

In practice, there is no need to list *all* the rows of Π. That is, the algorithm presented in Chapter 4 permits us to list only the rows of Π corresponding to the specific priority level under consideration. Thus, the initial tableau used in the solution process need only contain the first row of Π, or $\pi^{(1)T}$. We are now ready to proceed to the discussion of the solution procedure, as adapted to our specific tableau.

Steps of Solution Procedure

Our first step of the actual solution procedure for the previous example combines both steps 1 and 2 of the 8-step alogrithm of Chapter 4.

That is, we construct an initial tableau wherein our initial set of basic variables are the negative deviation variables of the LGP model (i.e., η_1, η_2, η_3, and η_4—which correspond to v_3, v_4, v_5, and v_6 of the general form). Corresponding to the basis is a basis inverse that is the identity matrix. We then compute β, $\pi^{(1)T}$ and u_1 as

$$\beta = B^{-1}\,b = \begin{pmatrix} 30 \\ 15 \\ 1000 \\ 40 \end{pmatrix}$$

$$\pi^{(1)T} = (0\ \ 0\ \ 0\ \ 0)\ \ B^{-1} = (0\ \ 0\ \ 0\ \ 0)$$

$$u_1 = c_B^{(1)T}\,B^{-1}\,b = \pi^{(1)T}\,b = 0$$

As a result, our initial tableau is given as

v_3	1	0	0	0	30
v_4	0	1	0	0	15
v_5	0	0	1	0	1000
v_6	0	0	0	1	40
$\pi^{(1)T}$	0	0	0	0	0

We are now ready to proceed to step 3 and compute $d_j^{(1)}$ for v_1, v_2, v_7, v_8, v_9, and v_{10} (i.e., for x_1, x_2, ρ_1, ρ_2, ρ_3, and ρ_4). These values are as follows:

$$d_1^{(1)} = \pi^{(1)T}\,a_1 - c_1^{(1)}$$

$$= (0\ \ 0\ \ 0\ \ 0)\begin{pmatrix} 1 \\ 0 \\ 8 \\ 1 \end{pmatrix} - 0 = 0$$

$$d_2^{(1)} = 0$$
$$d_7^{(1)} = -1$$
$$d_8^{(1)} = -1$$
$$d_9^{(1)} = 0$$
$$d_{10}^{(1)} = 0$$

Proceeding to step 4, we note that there are *no* positive valued $d_j^{(1)}$ elements (i.e., for the set of nonbasic and unchecked variables). Thus, we move to step 8.

The reader is now advised to pay particular attention to how step 8 is carried out, as it is especially tailored for our specific tableau. From step 8, we first note that neither stopping condition holds. Thus, we "check" variables v_7 and v_8.

v_7 (√)

v_8 (√)

Checked variables shall *never* be candidates to enter any subsequent basis (as their introduction would only serve to degrade the achievement of higher-level goals). Next, and although not specifically spelled out in the algorithm, we cross out the entire tableau row associated with $\pi^{(k)T}$ (i.e., $\pi^{(1)T}$ at this step). Finally, and still as a part of step 8, we set

$$k = k + 1 = 2$$

and then compute the entire *new* bottom row of the tableau as associated with rank or priority two. That is, we compute $\pi^{(2)T}$ and u_2 from the formulas previously specified.

Returning to step 2, the tableau now associated with this step is as shown below.

						(√)
v_3	1	0	0	0	30	v_7
v_4	0	1	0	0	15	v_8
v_5	0	0	1	0	1000	
v_6	0	0	0	1	40	
$\pi^{(2)T}$	0	0	1	0	1000	

The checked variables are now listed to the right of the tableau.

Moving to step 3, we compute the values of $d_j^{(2)}$ for v_1, v_2, v_9, and v_{10} (i.e., we do *not* evaluate these values for the checked variables). Thus:

$$d_1^{(2)} = 8 \qquad d_9^{(2)} = -1$$

$$d_2^{(2)} = 12 \qquad d_{10}^{(2)} = 0$$

Proceeding to step 4, we note that v_2 is selected as the entering variable. That is,

$$q = 2$$

We next update the entering column, $\boldsymbol{\alpha}_2$, in step 5:

$$\boldsymbol{\alpha}_q = \boldsymbol{\alpha}_2 = \mathbf{B}^{-1}\mathbf{a}_2 = \begin{pmatrix} 1 & 0 & 0 & 0 \\ 0 & 1 & 0 & 0 \\ 0 & 0 & 1 & 0 \\ 0 & 0 & 0 & 1 \end{pmatrix} \begin{pmatrix} 0 \\ 1 \\ 12 \\ 2 \end{pmatrix} = \begin{pmatrix} 0 \\ 1 \\ 12 \\ 2 \end{pmatrix} = \begin{pmatrix} \alpha_{1,2} \\ \alpha_{2,2} \\ \alpha_{3,2} \\ \alpha_{4,2} \end{pmatrix}$$

Moving to step 6, the leaving basic variable is determined. That is,

$$\frac{\beta_p}{\alpha_{p,2}} = \min\left\{\frac{\beta_1}{\alpha_{1,2}}, \frac{\beta_2}{\alpha_{2,2}}, \frac{\beta_3}{\alpha_{3,2}}, \frac{\beta_4}{\alpha_{4,2}}\right\}$$

$$\text{for } \alpha_{i,2} > 0$$

As a result, we see that $p = 2$. That is, the second basic variable ($v_{B,2}$) is the departing basic variable. From the tableau, we note that $v_{B,2}$ corresponds to v_4. Thus:

$v_{B,2} = v_4$, the *departing* variable
$v_q \;\; = v_2$, the *entering* variable

Before proceeding further, note that the previous steps 4 though 6 may be more conveniently carried out directly in conjunction with the tableau. Specifically, from step 5, we enter the updated $\boldsymbol{\alpha}_q$ ($\boldsymbol{\alpha}_2$ in this case) directly to the right of the matrix, as shown below.

	Basis Inverse				β	α_2	θ	(√)
v_3	1	0	0	0	30	0	–	v_7
v_4	0	1	0	0	15	(1)	15/1*	v_8
v_5	0	0	1	0	1000	12	1000/12	
v_6	0	0	0	1	40	2	40/2	
$\pi^{(2)T}$	0	0	1	0	1000	12		

Note that the "12" under $\boldsymbol{\alpha}_2$, and in the very bottom position, is the value of $d_2^{(2)}$ as computed in step 3. Directly to the right of the $\boldsymbol{\alpha}_2$ column is the column headed by "Θ," where

$$\Theta_i = \beta_i / \alpha_{i,q} \qquad \text{with } \alpha_{i,q} > 0 \qquad [5.7]$$

That is, Θ is simply the set of ratios from (4.26) and used to determine the departing basic variable. The Θ_i with the minimum ratio is denoted by an asterisk.

We are now ready for step 7, the pivoting operation. To accomplish this, we use the last tableau as listed above wherein q = 2, p = 2. Our so-called pivot element, $\alpha_{2,2} = 1$, is circled in this tableau. The purely mechanical procedure by which a new basis inverse may be formed is now described.

First, we define $\mathbf{B}^{-1}$ as the "old" basis inverse and $b_{i,j}$ as the element of $\mathbf{B}^{-1}$ in the ith row, j^{th} column. Correspondingly, $\hat{\mathbf{B}}^{-1}$ and $\hat{b}_{i,j}$ are the "new" basis inverse and new elements, respectively. To derive the new basis inverse, we use the following formulas:

$$\hat{b}_{p,j} = b_{p,j}/\alpha_{p,q} \qquad \forall j \tag{5.8}$$

$$\hat{b}_{i,j} = b_{i,j} - [(\alpha_{i,q})(b_{p,j})/\alpha_{p,q}] \tag{5.9}$$

$$\text{for } \forall i \text{ and } \forall j \qquad \text{but } i \neq p$$

Using these formulas plus those for computing u_k, $\boldsymbol{\beta}$, and $\pi^{(k)T}$, we develop the resultant new tableau, as shown below, and return to step 2.

	Basis Inverse				β	(√)
v_3	1	0	0	0	30	v_7
v_2	0	1	0	0	15	v_8
v_5	0	−12	1	0	820	
v_6	0	−2	0	1	10	
$\pi^{(2)T}$	0	−12	1	0	820	

Before proceeding to step 3, note carefully that v_2 has replaced v_4 (in the position of the second basic variable, $v_{B,2}$) in the above tableau.

Step 3.

$d_1^{(2)} = 8 \qquad d_9^{(2)} = -1$

$d_4^{(2)} = -12 \qquad d_{10}^{(2)} = 0$

Step 4. v_1 is the entering variable and q = 1.

Steps 5 and 6 are then summarized in the following tableau:

						α_1	θ	(√)
v_3	1	0	0	0	30	1	30/1	v_7
v_2	0	1	0	0	15	0	–	v_8
v_5	0	−12	1	0	820	8	820/8	
v_6	0	−2	0	1	10	(1)	10/1*	
$\pi^{(2)T}$	0	−12	1	0	820	8		

Consequently, v_6 (the smallest Θ ratio) is the departing variable and v_1 enters. This leads to the next tableau, via the pivoting process:

						(√)
v_3	1	2	0	−1	20	v_7
v_2	0	1	0	0	15	v_8
v_5	0	4	1	−8	740	
v_1	0	−2	0	1	10	
$\pi^{(2)T}$	0	4	1	−8	740	

Step 3. We determine that

$$d_4^{(2)} = 4 \qquad d_9^{(2)} = -1$$

$$d_6^{(2)} = -8 \qquad d_{10}^{(2)} = 8$$

Step 4. The entering variable is v_{10}, thus q = 10.

Steps 5 and 6 are again summarized in the tableau:

						α_{10}	θ	(√)
v_3	1	2	0	−1	20	(1)	20/1*	v_7
v_2	0	1	0	0	15	0	—	v_8
v_5	0	4	1	−8	740	8	740/8	
v_1	0	−2	0	1	10	−1	—	
$\pi^{(2)T}$	0	4	1	−8	740	8		

Thus, v_{10} enters and v_3 departs. The pivoting process then leads to the following tableau:

						(√)
v_{10}	1	2	0	−1	20	v_7
v_2	0	1	0	0	15	v_8
v_5	−8	−12	1	0	580	
v_1	1	0	0	0	30	
$\pi^{(2)T}$	−8	−12	1	0	580	

Step 3. We determine that

$$d_3^{(2)} = -8 \qquad d_6^{(2)} = 0$$
$$d_4^{(2)} = -12 \qquad d_9^{(2)} = -1$$

Step 4. No $d_j^{(2)}$ are positive so we go to step 8.

Step 8. Neither stopping rule is met so we check the variables v_3, v_4, and v_9. We also cross out the $\pi^{(2)T}$ row and set $k = k + 1 = 3$.

Step 2. The tableau now associated with the step is shown below:

						(√)
v_{10}	1	2	0	−1	20	v_7
v_2	0	1	0	0	15	v_8
v_5	−8	−12	1	0	580	v_3
v_1	1	0	0	0	30	v_4
$\pi^{(3)T}$	1	2	0	−1	20	v_9

Step 3. We next evaluate $d_j^{(3)}$ for all nonbasic, unchecked variables. That is,

$$d_6^{(3)} = -1$$

Step 4. Go to step 8.

Step 8. The first stopping condition of step 8 is satisfied. Thus, we stop with the optimal solution.

Listing the Results

Having followed the algorithm through to convergence, we are now, of course, concerned with determining the specific values associated with the solution. From the last tableau developed we may immediately read off the optimal program. That is,

$$v_{B,1} = v_{10}^* = 20 \qquad v_{B,3} = v_5^* = 580$$

$$v_{B,2} = v_2^* = 15 \qquad v_{B,4} = v_1^* = 30$$

Thus, in the original model

$$\rho_4^* = 20 \qquad \eta_3^* = 580$$

$$x_2^* = 15 \qquad x_1^* = 30$$

and all other variables are nonbasic, or zero valued. Alternatively, we could have computed $\mathbf{v}_B^*$ as

$$\mathbf{v}_B = \mathbf{B}^{-1}\,\mathbf{b} = \beta$$

and $\mathbf{v}_N = \mathbf{0}$ by definition.

The achievement vector is thus determined by

$$u_k = \mathbf{c}^{(k)T}\,\mathbf{B}^{-1}\,\mathbf{b} \qquad \forall k$$

and is

$$u_1^* = (0\ \ 0\ \ 0\ \ 0)\begin{pmatrix} 1 & 2 & 0 & -1 \\ 0 & 1 & 0 & 0 \\ -8 & -12 & 1 & 0 \\ 1 & 0 & 0 & 0 \end{pmatrix}\begin{pmatrix} 30 \\ 15 \\ 1000 \\ 40 \end{pmatrix} = 0$$

$$u_2^* = 580$$

$$u_3^* = 20$$

$$u_4^* = 0$$

And, in fact, all other information of interest (e.g., the shadow price vectors) may be similarly derived via a knowledge of $\mathbf{B}^{-1}$.

Additional Tableau Information

In Chapter 4, we discussed certain conditions associated with a basic solution. We now describe how these conditions may be detected via an examination of the tableaux used in algorithmic implementation.

Feasibility. The basis is feasible if and only if $\boldsymbol{\beta} \geq \mathbf{0}$. With LGP (except in certain special cases such as integer LGP and sensitivity analysis), we always start with a basic feasible solution, and via the examination of the Θ ratios never permit the basis to become infeasible. Consequently, if the right-hand side (i.e., $\boldsymbol{\beta}$) of the tableau ever includes a negative element, an error in computation is indicated. Note, however, that when using a digital computer, a β_i value of zero (which is acceptable), could be delivered as some very small *negative* value. Consequently, certain tolerances about zero are always maintained and any value within these tolerances is treated as a zero.

Implementability. As long as $u_1^* = 0$, the basic feasible solution is implementable. However, with LGP—and quite unlike LP—the solution process will continue even if $u_1 > 0$, and a solution as close to implementable as possible will be developed.

Optimality. In Chapter 4, we noted that a basic feasible solution is optimal whenever all shadow price vectors ($\mathbf{d}_j$), for nonbasic variables, are lexicographically nonpositive. Although this is true, we do not explicitly examine these vectors in our convergence check. Rather, this examination is achieved implicitly via step 8. As such, the optimality condition cannot *directly* be observed by simply examining the tableau we use.

Alternate optimal solutions. An alternate optimal solution is indicated when, in the *last* implementation of step 3, there is at least one shadow price element having a value of zero. That is, if some $d_j^{(k)} = 0$ for an unchecked and nonbasic variable in the last cycle through step 3, then there exists an alternate optimal solution (actually, an infinite number of alternate optimal solutions—and a finite number of alternate optimal basic feasible solutions). In our previous example, there were no alternate optimal solutions. Given an alternate optimal solution, this means that the set of optimal solutions to the LGP model may be encompassed *within* a region rather than strictly on the *boundary* of a region as is the case in conventional LP. Such a result is unique to GP and (despite certain protests by theoreticians) is, in fact, *an advantage* in the *practical* sense. That is, if a region exists wherein all solutions have the same $\mathbf{u}^*$, we have a variety of acceptable solutions to present to our decision maker. Further, as is well established, interior solutions are invariably more stable (i.e., less affected by variations in the model parameters) then are those on the boundaries.

Degeneracy. We observe a degenerate basic solution whenever any variable in the basis takes on a value of zero. Thus, in the tableau, we simply need to observe $\boldsymbol{\beta}$. Examining all the tableaux associated with our previous example, we see that degeneracy was never encountered. The importance of degeneracy was, until relatively recently, felt to be mainly of theoretical interest. Specifically, a few pathological examples were constructed where degeneracy led to a cycling phenomenon in the pivoting process. However, analysts now have observed such cycling in some real-world, large-scale problems and, in particular, in integer programming. Fortunately, there are practical ways to avoid or at least alleviate the problems associated with this condition (Charnes and Cooper, 1961; Lasdon, 1970; Murtagh, 1981).

Unbounded programs. As discussed in Chapter 4, the LGP achievement vector, $\mathbf{u}^T$, can never be unbounded. However, in certain cases the *program* may be (i.e., the value of some v_j—that is, nonbasic and unchecked—may approach infinity). This instance may be detected in the *final* tableau. If, for some v_j (where v_j is nonbasic and unchecked), *both* $d_j = 0$ (i.e., the d_j computed in the *last* implementation of step 3) and $\alpha_j \leq 0$, then an unbounded program exists. This may mean that the right-hand side of some goal could be increased (or decreased) without bound. If so, this situation may be examined via LGP sensitivity analysis.

Some Computational Considerations

The difference between the manner in which an algorithm is implemented by hand (i.e., as in the previous example or as is shown in virtually all textbook discussions) and how it is implemented on the computer can be quite vast. Only the most naive individual would expect to develop an *efficient* computer code by simply employing the steps outlined in a textbook algorithm. Further, the development of truly efficient computer software for LGP (or LP) implementation combines a great deal of art and experience, along with science. In this section we merely point out but a few factors to consider in computer implementation.

One of the guidelines typically used in model development (and which was employed in the previous example) is to "scale" the model. That is, the difference between the largest and smallest elements (i.e., $\mathbf{c}^{(k)}$, $\mathbf{A}$, $\mathbf{b}$) should be kept as small as possible. This serves to reduce computer rounding errors.

The actual growth of rounding errors should be monitored. One way is to simply, on some periodic basis, check the relation

$$\mathbf{A}\,\mathbf{v} = \mathbf{b}$$

We compute the value of the left-hand side (row by row) by using the original values of $\mathbf{A}$ in conjunction with the most recently computed values of $\mathbf{v}$. These results are then compared with the original set of $\mathbf{b}$. If differences are "significant" (that is, the accumulation of rounding errors exceeds certain prescribed limits), then the basis inverse, $\mathbf{B}^{-1}$, must be "cleaned up." This cleaning-up process is accomplished by a technique known as "reinversion" (Lasdon, 1970; Murtagh, 1981).

The pivoting process, particularly an unsophisticated one such as depicted in our example (see formulas 5.8 and 5.9), can contribute to rounding errors. That is, if $\alpha_{p,q}$ (the pivot element) is very small, its division into a relatively large numerator can create an extremely large number whose actual value must be substantially rounded off in the computer's representation of the number. As such, given a tie in entering or departing variables, one way to break the tie would be to favor the pivot having the largest pivot element.

Yet another consideration in the pivoting procedure is the choice of entering variables. Here we are *not* referring to a case in which ties for the most positive $d_j^{(k)}$ exist. Rather, the entering variable could be selected as one having a value of $d_j^{(k)}$ that is actually not the largest value. Further, such a choice *could* lead to convergence in fewer iterations and/or with less rounding error. In LP, numerous "pricing methods" (Murtagh, 1981) have been developed to accomplish such improvements and they could be used (and, in some cases, are being used) in LGP as well.

As one further comment in our brief survey of computational refinements, we note that the sometimes dazzling performance of LP or LGP codes is based on a critical assumption, that the matrix **A** is *sparse* (i.e., most elements are zeros). In fact, folklore amongst the LP analysts would have one conclude that such densities rarely exceed 5% and are, in most cases, less (or well less) than 1%. This myth continues to be perpetuated because most mathematical programming analysts (specifically those in the fields of operations research and management science) seem to religiously avoid problems in engineering design (where densities of 20% to even *100%* may exist). However, if one does indeed have a sparse problem (or chooses to confine his or her interests to such problems), then tremendous advances in computational performance are to be had. The most immediate of these, and most obvious, is in the realm of data storage. Commercial LP codes routinely use sophisticated data "packing" and "unpacking" algorithms to take advantage of sparsity. Taking a more brute force point of view, we note that the storage of the **A** matrix is usually best accomplished (and *always* best accomplished if the matrix is sparse) when **A** is stored column by column and only nonzero column entries are actually recorded.

Examining the steps of the algorithm, as listed in Chapter 4 (and as carried out in the example of this chapter), we can note that the bulk of operations are those in steps 3 and 7. However, inasmuch as in step 3 we perform the following:

$$d_j^{(k)} = \pi^{(k)T} \mathbf{a}_j - c_j^{(k)}$$

and $\mathbf{a}_j$ is assumed sparse, the number of operations (i.e., of an element in $\pi^{(k)T}$ with an element in $\mathbf{a}_j$) can be kept quite small if the operations are restricted to only those that involve nonzero elements in $\mathbf{a}_j$. This simple observation alone can provide tremendous reduction in computer time.

Bounded Variables

One relatively simple computational refinement, and one not discussed in the previous section, may be had if one is dealing with *bounded* variables (and, in particular, if there are a large number of such variables). Specifically, if some or all of the structural variables in the LGP model are bounded from above—for example, if

$$\mathbf{x}' \leq \mathbf{r} \quad \text{and} \quad \mathbf{x}' \in \mathbf{x}$$

where r_j is the upper bound on x_j', then one may take advantage of a slightly modified version of the 8-step algorithm and possibly achieve substantial savings in time and storage.

However, if one decides not to take special note of the bounded variables then $\mathbf{x}' \leq \mathbf{r}$ must be included in $\mathbf{A}\,\mathbf{v} \leq \mathbf{b}$. Such inclusion increases the number of rows in $\mathbf{A}$, which has a direct impact on both computation time and computer storage. Thus, in this section we shall deal directly with the bounded variable situation.

Prior to describing the revisions necessary to the algorithm, let us first examine the effects of bounded variables on the basic solution—if such bounds are *not* included in $\mathbf{A}$. Recall that the set of goals may be written as

$$\mathbf{B}\mathbf{v}_B + \mathbf{N}\mathbf{v}_N = \mathbf{b}$$

Let us then define the following:

s = the set of *nonbasic* variables at zero, and

s′ = the set of *nonbasic* variables at their upper bound.

Thus:

$\mathbf{N}_s$ = the columns of **A** associated with $\mathbf{v}_N \in S$

$\mathbf{N}_{s'}$ = the columns of **A** associated with $\mathbf{v}_N \in S'$

Then:

$$\mathbf{B}\mathbf{v}_B + \mathbf{N}_{s'}\,\mathbf{v}_{N(s')} + \mathbf{N}_s\,\mathbf{v}_{N(s)} = \mathbf{b}$$

and, letting $\mathbf{v}_{N(s)} = \mathbf{0}$

$$\mathbf{v}_B = \mathbf{B}^{-1}\,\mathbf{b} - \mathbf{B}^{-1}\,\mathbf{N}_{s'}\,\mathbf{v}_{N(s')}$$

That is, $\mathbf{v}_B$ is no longer simply equal to $\mathbf{B} = \mathbf{B}^{-1}\mathbf{b}$ if bounded variables are explicitly considered.

Not only is there a change in the way we compute $\mathbf{v}_B$, there must also be a change in the way entering and departing variables are determined. Rather than deriving these new rules, we shall simply list them in our modified algorithm steps.

The procedure to follow in the case of explicit consideration of bounded variables is as follows:

(1) Do *not* include the bounded condition in the goal set. That is, do not include $\mathbf{x}' \leq \mathbf{r}$ in $\mathbf{A}\ \mathbf{v} = \mathbf{b}$.

(2) Modify step 4 of the 8-step algorithm of Chapter 4 to read as follows:

Step 4 (revised for bounded variables). Examine those $d_j^{(k)}$ as computed in step 3. If:

(a) $v_j = 0$, then v_j is a candidate to enter the basis if $d_j^{(k)} > 0$;

(b) $v_j = r_j$, then v_j is a candidate to enter the basis if $d_j^{(k)} < 0$. If there are no candidates, proceed to step 8. Otherwise, select the candidate with the largest *absolute value* of $d_j^{(k)}$ to enter the basis. Designate the entering variables as v_q.

(3) Finally, we modify step 6 of the algorithm as listed below:

Step 6 (revised for bounded variables). If $v_q = 0$ then go to (a), below. Otherwise, if $v_q = r_q$, go to (b).

(a) Determine the leaving basic variable ($v_{B,p}$) by computing the following ratio for each row:

If $\alpha_{i,q} < 0$ then $\Theta_i = -(r_{B,i} - v_{B,i})/\alpha_{i,q}$;[10]

If $\alpha_{i,q} \geq 0$ then $\Theta_i = v_{B,i}/\alpha_{i,q}$.

Let row p be the row with the minimum Θ ratio. If $\Theta_p \geq r_q$, then v_q does not enter the basis but is set to its upper bound. Go to step 6(c). Otherwise, replace $v_{B,p}$ by v_q in the basis where

$$v_q = \Theta_p$$

and $\mathbf{v}_B$ is adjusted according to

$$v_B = \begin{cases} v_q; & i = p \\ v_{B,i} - \alpha_{i,q}\,\theta_p; & i \neq p \end{cases}$$

Now go to step 7.

(b) Determine the leaving basic variable by computing the following ratio for each row:

If $\alpha_{i,j} > 0$ then $\theta_i = (r_{B,i} - v_{B,i})/\alpha_{i,q}$;

If $\alpha_{i,q} < 0$ then $\theta_i = -v_{B,i}/\alpha_{i,q}$;

If $\alpha_{i,q} = 0$ then $\theta_i = \infty$.

Let row p be the row with the minimum Θ ratio. If $\Theta_p \geq r_q$, then v_q does not enter the basis but is set to zero and we proceed to step 6(c). Otherwise, replace $v_{B,p}$ by v_q in the basis where

$$v_q = r_q - \Theta_p$$

and $\mathbf{v}_B$ is adjusted according to

$$v_B = \begin{cases} v_q; & i = p \\ v_{B,i} + \alpha_{i,q}\,\theta_p; & i \neq p \end{cases}$$

Now go to step 7.

(c) Recompute $\mathbf{v}_B$ where

$$\mathbf{v}_B = \mathbf{B}^{-1}\,\mathbf{b} - \mathbf{B}^{-1}\,\mathbf{N}_{s'}\,\mathbf{v}_{N(s')}$$

and return to step 2.

In addition to following the procedure listed in the above three steps, it should be obvious that we must always keep a record of those variables that are at their upper bound. With these considerations in mind, one may employ the modified algorithm on LGP models having bounded variables.

Solution of LP and Minsum LGP Models

Although the focus of this work is on the lexicographic LGP model, it is stressed that the algorithm presented may also be used to solve numerous other multiobjective models as well as conventional LP models (Ignizio, 1976b, 1982, 1983c, forthcoming). As such, it provides a single approach for a host of models.

To use our algorithm for the solution of alternate models (e.g., LP and minsum LGP) requires that such models first be placed in the format given by (4.1)-(4.4). For example, the general form of the LP model, as shown below:

$$\text{minimize } \mathbf{d}^{T}\mathbf{x} \qquad [5.10]$$

s.t.

$$\mathbf{A}'\mathbf{x} \begin{matrix} \leq \\ = \\ \geq \end{matrix} \mathbf{b} \qquad [5.11]$$

$$\mathbf{x} > \mathbf{0} \qquad [5.12]$$

is converted to the form of (4.1)-(4.4) via the following steps:

(1) Each rigid constraint (of 5.11) is transformed into the GP format via the procedure summarized in Table 3.1 (i.e., negative and positive deviation variables are augmented to each constraint).
(2) The achievement vector is formed with the rigid constraints having first priority and the single objective having second priority.

As a result (5.10)-(5.12) becomes

Find **v** so as to

$$\text{lexmin } \mathbf{u}^{T} = \left\{ \sum_{i=1}^{m} (w_i^{-} \eta_i + w_i^{+} \rho_i),\ (d^{T}x) \right\} \qquad [5.13]$$

s.t.

$$A'x + n - \rho = b \qquad [5.14]$$

$$x,\ \eta,\ \rho \geqslant 0 \qquad [5.15]$$

where

$w_i^- =$ one if η_i is to be minimized, and zero otherwise.
$w_i^+ =$ one if ρ_8 is to be minimized, and zero otherwise.

Rather obviously, (5.13)-(5.15) is now in the form specified via (4.1)-(4.4).

We may then apply the 8-step algorithm of Chapter 4 to the model by simply modifying a single step. Specifically, step 6 is changed by noting that if there are *no* Θ_i ratios wherein $\alpha_{i,q} > 0$, we stop with an ***unbounded*** solution. That is, $\mathbf{d}^T\mathbf{x}$ is then unbounded.

Solution of the minsum (or Archimedean) LGP model is even more straightforward. Specifically, if the lexicographic LGP model has but *two* terms in $\mathbf{u}^T$, it is considered a minsum LGP model. That is:

u_1 = the term associated with all rigid constraints,
u_2 = the term associated with *all* soft goals, wherein they are weighted according to importance.

6. DUALITY AND SENSITIVITY ANALYSIS

When we solve a model—whatever type of model and with whatever algorithm—we are typically only roughly midphase in our overall process of analysis. That is, the solution derived for our lexicographic LGP model is only guaranteed to be valid for the specific, *deterministic* representation used. However, in the real world, the data collected to represent the model coefficients are typically only estimates. Further, there could be errors in the modeling process or, once the model has been built, the system it represents may change. As such, it is vital to at least examine the *impact* of such changes, errors, and/or estimates on the solution as derived via our algorithm.

In conventional linear programming, such impact, or sensitivity analysis, may be conducted in a straightforward manner via a systematic procedure. This ability is the result of two properties of LP: the fact that the model is linear and the existence of the LP dual. Further, this ability is of such power and importance that it alone can explain much of the reason for the popularity of LP. In fact, in many cases we transform nonlinear models to LP models (e.g., via various approximations) so as to take full advantage of the abilities of LP, and in particular its ability to provide a full analysis of sensitivity.

All of the abilities inherent in conventional LP are also inherent to lexicographic LGP, including the ability to perform a complete and comprehensive sensitivity analysis. Further, as is the case with LP, the existence of such sensitivity analysis is largely based upon the existence and exploitation of the dual of the lexicographic LGP model. Consequently, before describing sensitivity analysis in LGP, we shall first discuss the development of the LGP dual—the *multidimensional dual.*

Formulation of the Multidimensional Dual

By the late 1960s, I had developed a partial set of tools for sensitivity analysis in LGP. However, to complete the approach, it was necessary to construct a representation of the *dual* of the initial, or *primal* LGP model. By the early 1970s, this dual—which I denoted as the "multidimensional dual"—was established (Ignizio, 1974a, 1974b). However, most existing papers and textbook discussions of the multidimensional dual have been at a rather elementary level. As a consequence, in this work we now provide a concise but more complete and somewhat more rigorous development; one that lends itself to a wide range of both theoretical and practical extensions (Ignizio, 1974a, 1974b, 1979b, 1982a, 1983b, 1985a; Markowski and Ignizio, 1983a, 1983b). This development is based on the transformed form of the lexicographic LGP model (i.e., the primal) as given in (4.15)-(4.17) and repeated below.

LGP primal: Find $\mathbf{v}$ so as to

$$\text{lexmin } \mathbf{u}^{\mathrm{T}} = \Big\{ [\mathbf{c}_{\mathrm{B}}^{(1)\mathrm{T}} \boldsymbol{\beta} - (\boldsymbol{\pi}^{(1)\mathrm{T}} \mathbf{N} - \mathbf{c}_{\mathrm{N}}^{(1)\mathrm{T}}) \mathbf{v}_{\mathrm{N}}], \ldots, [\mathbf{c}_{\mathrm{B}}^{(\mathrm{K})\mathrm{T}} \boldsymbol{\beta} - (\boldsymbol{\pi}^{(\mathrm{K})\mathrm{T}} \mathbf{N} - \mathbf{c}_{\mathrm{N}}^{(\mathrm{K})\mathrm{T}}) \mathbf{v}_{\mathrm{N}}] \Big\} \qquad [6.1]$$

s.t.

$$\mathbf{v}_{\mathrm{B}} = \boldsymbol{\beta} - \mathbf{B}^{-1} \mathbf{N} \mathbf{v}_{\mathrm{N}} \qquad [6.2]$$

$$\mathbf{v} = \begin{pmatrix} \mathbf{v}_B \\ \hline \mathbf{v}_N \end{pmatrix} \geq \mathbf{0} \qquad [6.3]$$

If we recall that we may rewrite (6.2) as

$$\mathbf{B}\mathbf{v}_B + \mathbf{N}\mathbf{v}_N = \mathbf{b} \qquad [6.4]$$

then the dual of (6.1), (6.4), and (6.3) may immediately be written as follows:

LGP Multidimensional Dual: Find **Y** so as to

$$\text{lexmax } \mathbf{w} = \mathbf{b}^T \mathbf{Y} + \left\{ \mathbf{c}_B^{(1)T} \mathbf{B}^{-1} \mathbf{b}, \ldots, \mathbf{c}_B^{(K)T} \mathbf{B}^{-1} \mathbf{b} \right\} \qquad [6.5]$$

s.t.

$$\begin{pmatrix} \mathbf{B}^T \\ \hline \mathbf{N}^T \end{pmatrix} \mathbf{Y} \underset{\leftarrow}{\leq} \begin{pmatrix} \mathbf{0} \\ \hline \mathbf{c}_N^{(1)} - \mathbf{N}^T (\mathbf{B}^{-1})^T \mathbf{c}_B^{(1)} \end{pmatrix}, \ldots, \begin{pmatrix} \mathbf{0} \\ \hline \mathbf{c}_N^{(K)} - \mathbf{N}^T (\mathbf{B}^{-1})^T \mathbf{c}_B^{(K)} \end{pmatrix} \qquad [6.6]$$

and **Y** *unrestricted and multidimensional.* [6.7]

Those readers with a familiarity with LP will recognize that the development of the multidimensional dual, or MDD, from the LGP primal follows a set of rules similar to those used to form a conventional LP dual. However, there are several rather unusual features of the MDD that we shall now comment on.

First, note that the set of dual variables, **Y**, is a *matrix* rather than simply a vector. Further, each element of **Y**, designated as $y_i^{(k)}$, is unrestricted in sign. We thus define $y_i^{(k)}$ as follows:

$y_i^{(k)}$ = the ith dual variable for the kth right-hand side.

That is, there is a separate set (or vector) of such dual variables for *each* right-hand side of (6.6).

Second, we see that (6.5), the MDD "achievement function," is an ordered vector for which we seek the *lexicographic maximum*. Further, the "goal set" of (6.6) has *multiple and prioritized* right-hand sides. This last feature is also reflected in the use of the symbol "$\lneq$", for the lexicographic inequality, in (6.6).

Associated with the MDD is a set of conditions that *encompass* all those existing within conventional LP. For example, the dual of the LGP dual is the primal. (For the reader desiring further details, we recommend the following references: Ignizio, 1976b, 1982a, 1985a, forthcoming; Markowski and Ignizio, 1983a, 1983b.)

A Numerical Example

The mechanics of the development of the MDD may be most easily illustrated via an example. We thus list the following *primal* LGP model.

Find **x** so as to

$$\text{lexmin} \quad \mathbf{u}^T = \{(\rho_1 + \rho_2), (2\eta_3 + 3\eta_4)\} \qquad [6.8]$$

s.t.

$$\left.\begin{aligned} x_1 + \quad x_2 + \eta_1 - \rho_1 &= 12 \\ 2x_1 + \quad x_2 + \eta_2 - \rho_2 &= 20 \\ 16x_1 + 10x_2 + \eta_3 - \rho_3 &= 160 \\ 3x_1 + \ 5x_2 + \eta_4 - \rho_4 &= 60 \end{aligned}\right\} \qquad [6.9]$$

$$\mathbf{x}, \eta, \rho \geqslant \mathbf{0} \qquad [6.10]$$

wherein:

$$\begin{aligned} \mathbf{v}^T &= (x_1 \ x_2 \ \vdots \ \eta_1 \ \eta_2 \ \eta_3 \ \eta_4 \ \vdots \ \rho_1 \ \rho_2 \ \rho_3 \ \rho_4) \\ \mathbf{c}^{(1)T} &= (0 \ 0 \ \vdots \ 0 \ 0 \ 0 \ 0 \ \vdots \ 1 \ 1 \ 0 \ 0) \\ \mathbf{c}^{(2)T} &= (0 \ 0 \ \vdots \ 0 \ 0 \ 2 \ 3 \ \vdots \ 0 \ 0 \ 0 \ 0) \end{aligned}$$

and, because the initial basis always consists of the negative deviation variables:

$$\mathbf{B} = \begin{pmatrix} 1 & 0 & 0 & 0 \\ 0 & 1 & 0 & 0 \\ 0 & 0 & 1 & 0 \\ 0 & 0 & 0 & 1 \end{pmatrix} \qquad \mathbf{N} = \begin{pmatrix} 1 & 1 & -1 & 0 & 0 & 0 \\ 2 & 1 & 0 & -1 & 0 & 0 \\ 16 & 10 & 0 & 0 & -1 & 0 \\ 3 & 5 & 0 & 0 & 0 & -1 \end{pmatrix}$$

Using this, we may thus form the MDD as follows:

Find **Y** so as to

$$\text{lexmax } \mathbf{w} = (12 \quad 20 \quad 160 \quad 60)\mathbf{Y} + \{0,500\} \qquad [6.11]$$

s.t.

$$\begin{pmatrix} 1 & 0 & 0 & 0 \\ 0 & 1 & 0 & 0 \\ 0 & 0 & 1 & 0 \\ 0 & 0 & 0 & 1 \\ \hdashline 1 & 2 & 16 & 3 \\ 1 & 1 & 10 & 5 \\ -1 & 0 & 0 & 0 \\ 0 & -1 & 0 & 0 \\ 0 & 0 & -1 & 0 \\ 0 & 0 & 0 & -1 \end{pmatrix} \mathbf{Y} \underset{\leftarrow}{\leq} \left(\begin{pmatrix} 0 \\ 0 \\ 0 \\ 0 \\ \hdashline 0 \\ 0 \\ 1 \\ 1 \\ 0 \\ 0 \end{pmatrix}, \begin{pmatrix} 0 \\ 0 \\ 0 \\ 0 \\ \hdashline -41 \\ -35 \\ 0 \\ 0 \\ 2 \\ 3 \end{pmatrix} \right) \qquad [6.12]$$

and **Y** multidimensional and unrestricted. [6.13]

The reader should note in particular that the following relationships were used to construct the above dual form:

$$\mathbf{c}_B^{(1)T} = (0 \;\; 0 \;\; 0 \;\; 0) \qquad \mathbf{c}_B^{(2)T} = (0 \;\; 0 \;\; 2 \;\; 3)$$
$$\mathbf{c}_N^{(1)T} = (0 \;\; 0 \;\; 1 \;\; 1 \;\; 0 \;\; 0) \qquad \mathbf{c}_N^{(2)T} = (0 \;\; 0 \;\; 0 \;\; 0 \;\; 0 \;\; 0)$$

Using any algorithm for solution to the MDD (Ignizio, 1976b, 1982a, 1985a), we would find that the optimal MDD program is given as

$$\mathbf{Y}^* = \begin{pmatrix} 0 & -75/3 \\ 0 & 0 \\ 0 & -1 \\ 0 & 0 \end{pmatrix}$$

That is, the solution to the model for the first right-hand side (i.e., priority) is

$$y_1^{(1)*} = 0$$
$$y_2^{(1)*} = 0 \qquad \text{and } w^{(1)*} = 0$$
$$y_3^{(1)*} = 0$$
$$y_4^{(1)*} = 0$$

For the second right-hand side, we have

$$y_1^{(2)*} = -75/3$$
$$y_2^{(2)*} = 0 \qquad \text{and } w^{(2)*} = 40$$
$$y_3^{(2)*} = -1$$
$$y_4^{(2)*} = 0$$

In a subsequent section, we shall see how such results may be obtained.

Interpretation of the Dual Variables

The dual variables, **Y**, are interpreted in a manner essentially the same as employed in conventional linear programming. That is, the solution to the MDD given in the previous section was

$$\mathbf{Y}^* = \begin{pmatrix} 0 & -75/3 \\ 0 & 0 \\ 0 & -1 \\ 0 & 0 \end{pmatrix}$$

If we were to solve the *primal* of the above problem, we would find that the shadow price vectors for each original basic variable (i.e., the η terms or v_3 through v_6) are

$$(\eta_1): \quad \mathbf{d}_3 = \begin{pmatrix} 0 \\ -75/3 \end{pmatrix}$$

$$(\eta_2):\quad \mathbf{d}_4 = \begin{pmatrix} 0 \\ 0 \end{pmatrix}$$

$$(\eta_3):\quad \mathbf{d}_5 = \begin{pmatrix} 0 \\ -1 \end{pmatrix}$$

$$(\eta_4):\quad \mathbf{d}_6 = \begin{pmatrix} 0 \\ 0 \end{pmatrix}$$

Thus, the first row of **Y*** corresponds to the shadow price vector for η_1, the second row to the shadow price vector for η_2, and so on.

As a result, we see that $y_i^{(k)}$ is the per unit contribution of resource i (of the primal) to the kth term of the achievement function. For example, by noting that

$$y_1^{(1)} = 0 \quad \text{and} \quad y_1^{(2)} = -75/3$$

we see that an increase of one unit to b_1 (where $b_1 = 12$) in (6.9) will result in

(a) no impact on u_1, or implementability, and

(b) an improvement (i.e., reduction) in u_2 of $-75/3$ for every unit that b_1 is increased.

These observations are true only as long as the final (optimal) basis remains unchanged. We shall discuss how such ranges may be determined later in the chapter.

Solving the Multidimensional Dual

In sensitivity analysis for LGP, it is not absolutely essential that one know how to solve the MDD—to obtain the solution simply listed in the previous section. However, for completeness in presentation we provide, in this section, a brief description of one relatively recent and particularly efficient way to obtain the solution to the MDD (and, as a result, also obtain the solution to the primal). I have designated this method as the sequential MDD simplex algorithm (Ignizio, 1985a). One particularly interesting feature of this approach is that the MDD is solved via the solution of a *sequence* of conventional LP models.

Further, each LP model in the sequence typically is considerably smaller than its predecessor. We list the steps of this algorithm as follows:

Step 1. Establish the multidimensional dual as given in (6.5)-(6.7). Set k = 1.

Step 2. Form the LP model from (6.5)-(6.7) that includes only the kth right-hand side vector of (6.6). Solve using any conventional simplex algorithm. If k = K, go to step 4. Otherwise, go to step 3.

Step 3. For the linear programming model previously solved, remove all *nonbinding* constraints (this is analogous to the nonbasic variable "checking" procedure in the algorithm for the primal). If the subsequent model has *no* constraints, go to step 4. Otherwise, set k = k + 1 and return to step 2.

Step 4. The present solution is that which is optimal for the MDD and the kth right-hand side. The corresponding optimal solution to the *primal* model is given by the shadow prices as associated with the initial set of basic variables for the kth dual model.

To illustrate, we shall solve the LGP model given in primal form in (6.8)-(6.10) and in MDD form in (6.11)-(6.13). The first LP model to be solved is thus:

$$\text{maximize } w^{(1)} = 12y_1^{(1)} + 20y_2^{(1)} + 160y_3^{(1)} + 60y_4^{(1)} + \{0\}$$

s.t.

$$\begin{pmatrix} 1 & 0 & 0 & 0 \\ 0 & 1 & 0 & 0 \\ 0 & 0 & 1 & 0 \\ 0 & 0 & 0 & 1 \\ \hdashline 1 & 2 & 16 & 3 \\ 1 & 1 & 10 & 5 \\ -1 & 0 & 0 & 0 \\ 0 & -1 & 0 & 0 \\ 0 & 0 & -1 & 0 \\ 0 & 0 & 0 & -1 \end{pmatrix} y^{(1)} \leqslant \begin{pmatrix} 0 \\ 0 \\ 0 \\ 0 \\ \hdashline 0 \\ 0 \\ 1 \\ 1 \\ 0 \\ 0 \end{pmatrix}$$

and $y^{(1)}$ unrestricted.

We may note that the first four constraints in conjunction with the last four simply denote upper and lower bounds on $\mathbf{y}^{(1)}$. Solving this problem via any conventional LP algorithm, we obtain

$$\mathbf{y}^{(1)*} = \begin{pmatrix} 0 \\ 0 \\ 0 \\ 0 \end{pmatrix} \qquad \text{and } w^{(1)*} = 0 + \{0\} = 0$$

Further, for this solution, both the seventh and eighth constraints are nonbinding and thus may be dropped from the LP model for k = 2. The next, and final LP model in the sequence is thus:

$$\text{maximize } w^{(2)} = 12y_1^{(2)} + 20y_2^{(2)} + 160y_3^{(2)} + 60y_4^{(2)} + \{500\}$$

s.t.

$$\begin{pmatrix} 1 & 0 & 0 & 0 \\ 0 & 1 & 0 & 0 \\ 0 & 0 & 1 & 0 \\ 0 & 0 & 0 & 1 \\ 1 & 2 & 16 & 3 \\ 1 & 1 & 10 & 5 \\ 0 & 0 & -1 & 0 \\ 0 & 0 & 0 & -1 \end{pmatrix} \mathbf{y}^{(2)} \leqslant \begin{pmatrix} 0 \\ 0 \\ 0 \\ 0 \\ -41 \\ -35 \\ 2 \\ 3 \end{pmatrix}$$

and $\mathbf{y}^{(2)}$ unrestricted.

Again, solving via any LP simplex algorithm we obtain

$$\mathbf{y}^{(2)*} = \begin{pmatrix} -75/3 \\ 0 \\ -1 \\ 0 \end{pmatrix} \qquad \text{and } \mathbf{w}^{(2)*} = -460 + \{500\} = 40$$

Further, from the shadow prices for the final LP tableau, we may determine that the optimal primal program is

$$\mathbf{x}^* = \begin{pmatrix} 20/3 \\ 16/3 \end{pmatrix} \qquad \text{and } \mathbf{u}^T = (0, 40)$$

In actual practice, the Sequential MDD Simplex algorithm may be enhanced by numerous simplifications (Ignizio, 1983a, 1985a, forthcoming) and thus the algorithm provides exceptionally good computational performance. In fact, when comparisons were made with the very latest version of the Sequential LGP, or SLGP method (a *primal* based method discussed briefly in Chapter 2), the dual based scheme was substantially superior.

A Special MDD Simplex Algorithm

The algorithm discussed above may be used to solve *any* LGP model (i.e., in its MDD form). In this section we discuss a far more restricted dual based algorithm that will be of considerable use in certain, very special situations (Ignizio, 1974a, 1974b, 1976b, 1982a). Included among such special situations is that of LGP sensitivity analysis.

To use this special algorithm we must satisfy the following conditions with regard to the LGP *primal*:

(1) at least one element in $\mathbf{v}_B$ (i.e., $\boldsymbol{\beta}$) must be negative, and

(2) all shadow price column vectors, $\mathbf{d}_j$, must be lexicographically nonpositive.

Given these conditions, the algorithm listed below may be employed so as to *regain feasibility while maintaining the optimality condition.*

Step 1. Select the row with the most negative $v_{B,i}$ element. The basic variable associated with this row is the departing variable. Denote this row as i = p. Ties may be arbitrarily broken.

Step 2. Develop the pricing vectors *for all k*:

$$\boldsymbol{\pi}^{(k)T} = \mathbf{c}_B^{(k)T}\,\mathbf{B}^{-1} \qquad \forall k$$

Step 3. Price out all nonbasic columns, *for all levels of k*:

$$d_j^{(k)} = \boldsymbol{\pi}^{(k)T}\,\mathbf{a}_j - c_j^{(k)} \qquad \forall k$$

Step 4. Compute $\alpha_{p,j}$ for all (nonbasic) j:

$$\alpha_{p,j} = \mathbf{b}_p' \mathbf{a}_j \qquad [6.14]$$

where

$\mathbf{b}_p'$ = the pth row of $\mathbf{B}^{-1}$

$\mathbf{a}_j$ = the jth column of $\mathbf{A}$

Step 5. Determine the nonbasic variable associated with the lexicographically minimum "column ratio" where this column ratio is given by

$$\mathbf{r}_j = \begin{pmatrix} d_j^{(1)}/\alpha_{p,j} \\ \vdots \\ d_j^{(K)}/\alpha_{p,j} \end{pmatrix} \quad \text{for } \alpha_{p,j} < 0 \qquad [6.15]$$

Designate the nonbasic variable with the lexicographically minimum $\mathbf{r}_j$ as being column j = q. Ties may be arbitrarily broken.

Step 6. Using the pivoting procedure, exchange the entering variable for the departing variable and develop the new tableau.

Step 7. Repeat steps 1 through 6 until all $v_{B,i}$ are nonnegative.

To demonstrate the employment of the above algorithm, we shall use the example given below:

$$\text{lexmin } \mathbf{u}^T = \{(\rho_1 + \rho_2), (\eta_3), (\rho_4)\}$$

s.t.

$$\begin{aligned} x_1 + x_2 + \eta_1 - \rho_1 &= 10 \\ x_1 + \eta_2 - \rho_2 &= 12 \\ 5x_1 + 3x_2 + \eta_3 - \rho_3 &= 56 \\ x_1 + x_2 + \eta_4 - \rho_4 &= 12 \\ \mathbf{x}, \eta, \rho &\geq 0 \end{aligned}$$

A basic solution to this model is shown in the tableau below. Note carefully that, although basic, the program is *infeasible*.

	Basis Inverse				β
v_2	1	−1	0	0	−2
v_1	0	1	0	0	12
v_5	−3	−2	1	0	2
v_6	−1	0	0	1	2
$\pi^{(1)T}$	0	0	0	0	0
$\pi^{(2)T}$	−3	−2	1	0	2
$\pi^{(3)T}$	0	0	0	0	0

Using $\pi^{(k)T}$, we may compute all $\mathbf{d}_j$ (for $j \in N$):

$$\mathbf{d}_3 = \begin{pmatrix} 0 \\ -3 \\ 0 \end{pmatrix} \quad \mathbf{d}_4 = \begin{pmatrix} 0 \\ -2 \\ 0 \end{pmatrix} \quad \mathbf{d}_7 = \begin{pmatrix} -1 \\ 3 \\ 0 \end{pmatrix}$$

$$\mathbf{d}_8 = \begin{pmatrix} -1 \\ 2 \\ 0 \end{pmatrix} \quad \mathbf{d}_9 = \begin{pmatrix} 0 \\ -1 \\ 0 \end{pmatrix} \quad \mathbf{d}_{10} = \begin{pmatrix} 0 \\ 0 \\ -1 \end{pmatrix}$$

We thus note that this tableau does satisfy the two conditions for the employment of the special MDD simplex algorithm. That is, $v_{B,1} = v_2 = -2$ and all $\mathbf{d}_j$ are lexicographically nonpositive.

Proceeding through the steps of the algorithm, we note that $v_{B,1}$ (i.e., $\beta_1 = v_2$) is the departing variable and thus $i = p = 1$. Moving to step 4 we may then compute all $\alpha_{p,j}$ via (6.14). Step 4 leads to:

$$\alpha_{1,3} = 1 \quad \alpha_{1,4} = -1 \quad \alpha_{1,7} = -1$$

$$\alpha_{1,8} = 1 \quad \alpha_{1,9} = 0 \quad \alpha_{1,10} = 0$$

Because $\alpha_{1,4}$ and $\alpha_{1,7}$ are the only α-values that are negative, we need only compute the column ratios associated with v_4 and v_7. These are as follows:

$$\mathbf{r}_4^T = (0/-1, -2/-1, 0/-1) = (0,2,0)$$

$$\mathbf{r}_7^T = (-1/-1, 3/-1, 0/-1) = (1,-3,0)$$

Thus, $\mathbf{r}_4$ is the minimum column ratio and so v_4 ($j = q = 4$) is the entering variable. Letting $v_{B,1} = v_2$ depart and v_4 enter, our new tableau becomes

	Basis Inverse				$\boldsymbol{\beta}$
v_4	−1	1	0	0	2
v_1	1	0	0	0	10
v_5	−5	0	1	0	6
v_6	−1	0	0	1	2

Since $\boldsymbol{\beta} \geq \mathbf{0}$, this new solution is now feasible *and* optimal.

Discrete Sensitivity Analysis

We are now ready to proceed to our presentation of sensitivity analysis in LGP (Ignizio, 1982a). We begin this with a discussion of how *discrete* changes in the original LGP model are dealt with. We consider:

- a change in some $c_j^{(k)}$,
- a change in some b_i,
- a change in some $a_{i,j}$,
- the inclusion of a new structural variable, and
- the inclusion of a new goal or rigid constraint.

We shall consider, in turn, how each one of these changes may be dealt with. However, let us first note that we shall place a caret over the *new* parameter so as to distinguish its new value from its original value.

A change in some $c_j^{(k)}$. To determine the impact of a change in the value of some $c_j^{(k)}$ we must first determine if x_j is presently a basic or nonbasic variable. That is, if x_j is *nonbasic* and $c_j^{(k)}$ is changed to $\hat{c}_j^{(k)}$ then:

$$\hat{d}_j^{(k)} = \mathbf{c}_B^{(k)T}\, \mathbf{B}^{-1}\, \mathbf{a}_j - \hat{c}_j^{(k)}$$

That is, the only result of such a change is its impact on a *single* shadow price vector element. However, this could result in a solution that is now not optimal and the optimizing algorithm must then be continued.

If, however, $c_j^{(k)}$ is associated with some x_j that is basic, we affect an entire set of shadow price elements (i.e., all those at level k) plus we may change the value of u_k. That is, if x_j is *basic* and $c_j^{(k)}$ is changed to $\hat{c}_j^{(k)}$ then:

$$\hat{d}_j^{(k)} = \hat{\mathbf{c}}_B^{(k)T}\, \mathbf{B}^{-1}\, \mathbf{a}_j - c_j^{(k)} \qquad \text{for all } j \in N$$

and

$$\hat{u}_k = \hat{\mathbf{c}}_B^{(k)T}\, \mathbf{B}^{-1}\, \mathbf{b}$$

A change in some b_i. The change of some element of the original right-hand side vector is felt on $\boldsymbol{\beta}$ and $\mathbf{u}$. That is, if b_i is changed to b_i then:

$$\hat{\boldsymbol{\beta}} = \mathbf{B}^{-1}\, \hat{\mathbf{b}}$$

and

$$\hat{u}_k = \mathbf{c}_{\beta}^{(k)T}\, \mathbf{B}^{-1}\, \hat{\mathbf{b}}$$

As $\boldsymbol{\beta}$ can change, it can actually contain one or more *negative* elements. In this case, our special MDD simplex algorithm may be employed to regain feasibility.

A change in some $a_{i,j}$. The manner in which a change in $a_{i,j}$ (the "technological coefficients") is dealt with depends on whether x_j is basic or nonbasic. If x_j is basic we can proceed through a long and rather cumbersome procedure to determine the impact. Some analysts feel that it may be better simply to resolve the problem from the beginning. Consequently, we shall only describe the process used when x_j is nonbasic. That is, if x_j is *nonbasic* and $a_{i,j}$ is changed to $\hat{a}_{i,j}$ then:

$$\hat{\boldsymbol{\alpha}}_j = \mathbf{B}^{-1}\, \hat{\mathbf{a}}_j$$

and

$$\hat{d}_j^{(k)} = \mathbf{c}_B^{(k)T}\, \hat{\boldsymbol{\alpha}}_j - c_j^{(k)} \qquad \text{for all } k$$

Thus, if some $a_{i,j}$ (x_j nonbasic) is changed the entire $\boldsymbol{\alpha}_j$ vector may change and, in addition, an entire shadow price vector could also change. Thus, a change in $a_{i,j}$ may affect the optimality of a solution.

Adding a new structural variable. The addition of some new structural variable, x_j, has an impact identical to that of a change in an $a_{i,j}$ as associated with a nonbasic variable. That is, we may think of the $\mathbf{a}_j$ vector for the new variable as having previously been $\mathbf{0}$. We then compute the new $\boldsymbol{\alpha}_j$ and $d_j^{(k)}$ values as noted directly above. The result will be that either the present basis is still optimal or that it is not. In the first case this indicates that the new variable should not enter the basis whereas in the second we note that the new variable will improve the present solution.

Adding a new goal. The addition of a new goal (whether it is flexible or a rigid constraint) requires somewhat more work than was required for the previous changes. First, if some new goal, say G_r, is added to the lexicographic LGP model we must make sure that (for other than the case of rigid constraints) it is commensurable with all other goals at the priority level in which it is included. Second, the new goal will increase the size of the basis by one row and column. Third, to determine the new basis, we must first "operate" on the new goal so as to eliminate the coefficients of any basic variable from the goal. This can be accomplished via ordinary row operations. Finally, the inclusion of the new goal can affect both the feasibility and/or optimality of the present solution.

Parametric LGP

The previous discussion focused solely on *discrete* modifications to the original LGP model. In this section we shall briefly examine *parametric* LGP, or the investigation of changes over a *continuous range* (Ignizio, 1982a). In doing so, we shall confine our presentation to just parametric changes in b_i (i.e., the original right-hand-side value of goal i) and $c_j^{(k)}$ (the original weight or coefficient of variable j at the kth priority level). We shall deal with this latter case first.

A parameter in the achievement function. The easiest way to explain the approach used is via a simple numerical example. We shall use the following LGP model:

$$\text{lexmin } \mathbf{u}^T = \{(\rho_1 + \rho_2),\ (\eta_3 + 2\eta_4),\ (\eta_1)\}$$

s.t.

$$\begin{aligned} x_1 \qquad\quad + \eta_1 - \rho_1 &= 20 \\ x_2 + \eta_2 - \rho_2 &= 35 \\ -5x_1 + 3x_2 + \eta_3 - \rho_3 &= 220 \\ x_1 - x_2 + \eta_4 - \rho_4 &= 60 \\ \mathbf{x}, \eta, \rho &\geqslant \mathbf{0} \end{aligned}$$

Rewriting this model in general form we have

$$\text{lexmin } \mathbf{u}^T = \left\{\mathbf{c}^{(1)T}\mathbf{v},\ \mathbf{c}^{(2)T}\mathbf{v},\ \mathbf{c}^{(3)T}\mathbf{v}\right\}$$

s.t.

$$\mathbf{A}\mathbf{v} = \mathbf{b}$$

$$\mathbf{v} = \begin{pmatrix} \mathbf{v}_B \\ \hdashline \mathbf{v}_N \end{pmatrix} \geqslant \mathbf{0}$$

where

$$\mathbf{v}^T = (x_1\ x_2 \ \vdots\ \eta_1\ \eta_2\ \eta_3\ \eta_4\ \vdots\ \rho_1\ \rho_2\ \rho_3\ \rho_4)$$

or

$$\mathbf{v}^T = (v_1\ v_2\ \vdots\ v_3\ v_4\ v_5\ v_6\ \vdots\ v_7\ v_8\ v_9\ v_{10})$$

$$\mathbf{c}^{(1)T} = (0\ \ 0\ \vdots\ 0\ \ 0\ \ 0\ \ 0\ \vdots\ 1\ \ 1\ \ 0\ \ 0\ )$$

$$\mathbf{c}^{(2)T} = (0\ \ 0\ \vdots\ 0\ \ 0\ \ 1\ \ 2\ \vdots\ 0\ \ 0\ \ 0\ \ 0\ )$$

$$\mathbf{c}^{(3)T} = (0\ \ 0\ \vdots\ 1\ \ 0\ \ 0\ \ 0\ \vdots\ 0\ \ 0\ \ 0\ \ 0\ )$$

$$\mathbf{A} = \begin{pmatrix} 1 & 0 & 1 & 0 & 0 & 0 & -1 & 0 & 0 & 0 \\ 0 & 1 & 0 & 1 & 0 & 0 & 0 & -1 & 0 & 0 \\ -5 & 3 & 0 & 0 & 1 & 0 & 0 & 0 & -1 & 0 \\ 1 & -1 & 0 & 0 & 0 & 1 & 0 & 0 & 0 & -1 \end{pmatrix} \quad \mathbf{b} = \begin{pmatrix} 20 \\ 35 \\ 220 \\ 60 \end{pmatrix}$$

We first determine the optimal solution to the above model. The result is given in the tableau below:

	Basis Inverse				β
v_3	1	0	0	0	20
v_2	0	1	0	0	35
v_5	0	−3	1	0	115
v_6	0	1	0	1	95
$\pi^{(1)T}$	0	0	0	0	0
$\pi^{(2)T}$	0	−1	1	2	305
$\pi^{(3)T}$	1	0	0	0	20

In the original model above, the coefficient of v_6 (i.e., η_4) at priority level 2 (k = 2) was "2." Let us now determine the range of values for this coefficient over which the above program is still optimal. Thus, in place of $c_6^{(2)}$ we shall use a parameter, say "t." This results in a change in $\pi^{(2)T}$ for the above tableau. That is,

$$\hat{\pi}^{(2)T} = \hat{c}_B^{(2)T}\, B^{-1} = (0 \quad 0 \quad 1 \quad t)\begin{pmatrix} 1 & 0 & 0 & 0 \\ 0 & 1 & 0 & 0 \\ 0 & -3 & 1 & 0 \\ 0 & 1 & 0 & 1 \end{pmatrix}$$

or $$\hat{\pi}^{(2)T} = (0 \quad -3+t \quad 1 \quad t)$$

Using the new value of $\pi^{(2)T}$ we may compute the shadow price column vectors for all nonbasic variables. This results in

$$d_1 = \begin{pmatrix} 0 \\ -5+t \\ 1 \end{pmatrix} \qquad d_4 = \begin{pmatrix} 0 \\ -3+t \\ 0 \end{pmatrix} \qquad d_7 = \begin{pmatrix} -1 \\ 0 \\ -1 \end{pmatrix}$$

$$d_8 = \begin{pmatrix} -1 \\ 3-t \\ 0 \end{pmatrix} \qquad d_9 = \begin{pmatrix} 0 \\ -1 \\ 0 \end{pmatrix} \qquad d_{10} = \begin{pmatrix} 0 \\ -t \\ 0 \end{pmatrix}$$

Now, in order for the previous program to be optimal, all $\mathbf{d}_j$ must be lexicographically nonpositive, or

$$-5 + t < 0$$

$$-3 + 5 \leq 0$$

$$-t \leq 0$$

And these three relationships are simultaneously satisfied only when

$$0 \leq t \leq 3$$

Thus, as long as all other parameters remain unchanged, the weight on η_4 at priority level 2 may vary from 0 up to 3 and the original program will still be optimal. Using the same process, we could examine, *one at a time*, all of the remaining achievement function parameters. However, it should be obvious to the reader that the only other parameter of interest in *this* model would be the weight associated with η_3 at priority level 2.

A parameter in the right-hand side. A parameter in the achievement function must be examined for that range over which the original program is still *optimal.* A parameter in the right-hand side, however, will be examined for the range over which the original program is still *feasible.* To demonstrate, let us examine the range of values of b_1 for which the original program remains feasible. That is, we replace 20 (i.e., the value of b_1) by "t." Using the approach discussed earlier to investigate a discrete change in b_i, we find:

$$\hat{\boldsymbol{\beta}} = \mathbf{B}^{-1}\hat{\mathbf{b}} = \begin{pmatrix} 1 & 0 & 0 & 0 \\ 0 & 1 & 0 & 0 \\ 0 & -3 & 1 & 0 \\ 0 & 1 & 0 & 1 \end{pmatrix} \begin{pmatrix} t \\ 35 \\ 220 \\ 60 \end{pmatrix} = \begin{pmatrix} t \\ 35 \\ 115 \\ 95 \end{pmatrix}$$

And this new $\boldsymbol{\beta}$ is feasible as long as $0 \leq t < \infty$.

Next, examine the range on b_3. That is, we replace b_3 by t and determine the new right-hand side:

$$\hat{\boldsymbol{\beta}} = \begin{pmatrix} 1 & 0 & 0 & 0 \\ 0 & 1 & 0 & 0 \\ 0 & -3 & 1 & 0 \\ 0 & 1 & 0 & 1 \end{pmatrix} \begin{pmatrix} 20 \\ 35 \\ t \\ 60 \end{pmatrix} = \begin{pmatrix} 20 \\ 35 \\ t-105 \\ 95 \end{pmatrix}$$

and this is feasible as long as $t - 105 \geq 0$. Thus, the range on b_3 is

$$105 \leq t < \infty$$

Again, we can perform such an analysis on any or all of the right-hand side elements.

7. EXTENSIONS

In this volume, our attention has been focused, at least for the most part, on lexicographic linear goal programming (i.e., LGP with a preemptive priority structure, or non-Archimedean weights). However, even with this seemingly narrow perspective, we have seen that the methodology presented may also be *directly* applied to:

- lexicographic linear goal programming,
- minsum (or Archimedean) linear goal programming, and
- conventional linear programming.

In addition, with but minor modification we may extend our approach to encompass even further alternative methods for multiobjective optimization including fuzzy programming, fuzzy goal programming, and the generating method (Ignizio, 1979, 1981a, 1982b, 1983b; Ignizio and Daniels, 1983; Ignizio and Thomas, 1984; Yu, 1977; Zimmermann, 1978). As such, the methodology thus far presented provides an approach to either single-objective linear programming or most classes of multiple objective *linear* mathematical programming.

Goal programming (recall our discussion in Chapter 2) is not, however, limited to linear systems. Rather, powerful extensions of the GP concept exist and find real-world application in both integer and nonlinear models. In this section we shall very briefly discuss a few of these extensions so that the reader has at least some familiarity with other than strictly linear GP models. In addition, to conclude this chapter, we shall describe *interactive* approaches via GP, a topic of some considerable recent interest.

Integer GP

Sequential integer goal programming. Among the first approaches to integer GP, or IGP, was the so called sequential GP approach. This sequential approach was first proposed and developed by Ignizio and Huss in 1967 for the solution of strictly *linear* GP models (Ignizio, 1967, 1982a, 1983c; Ignizio and Perlis, 1979; Markowski and Ignizio, 1983b). However, there is no reason why the concept cannot be used in IGP or even in nonlinear GP (NLGP) and, in fact, it often finds such application. The basic thrust of sequential GP is to partition the GP model into a *related* sequence of conventional, or single-objective models. The general algorithm for sequential GP is given below.

Step 1. Establish the GP formulation of the model and set k = 1 (where K = total number of priority levels in **u**).

Step 2. Establish the mathematical model for *priority level 1 only.* That is,

$$\text{minimize } \mathbf{u}_1 = \mathbf{c}^{(1)T}\mathbf{v}$$

s.t.

$$f_i(x) + \eta_i - \rho_i = b_i \qquad \text{for } i \epsilon P_1 \textit{ only}$$

$$\mathbf{v} \geqslant \mathbf{0}$$

Step 3. Solve the single-objective problem associated with priority level k via any appropriate algorithm.[11] Let the optimal solution be designated as u_k^*.

Step 4. Set k = k + 1. If k > K, go to step 6. Otherwise, go to step 5.

Step 5. Establish the equivalent single-objective model for the next priority level (level k). This model is given as

$$\text{minimize } u_k = \mathbf{c}^{(k)T}\mathbf{v}$$

s.t.

$$f_i(x) + \eta_i - \rho_i = b_i \qquad \text{for } i \epsilon P_1 \cup P_2 \ldots \cup P_k{}^{12}$$

$$\mathbf{c}^{(s)T}\mathbf{v} = u_s^* \qquad \text{for } s = 1, 2, \ldots, k-1$$

$$\mathbf{v} \geqslant \mathbf{0}$$

and then proceed to step 3.

Step 6. The solution vector **v***, as associated with the last single-objective model is the optimal solution to the original GP model.

Note carefully that this algorithm as presented is applicable to *any* type of GP model (i.e., linear, integer, or nonlinear). A number of organizations utilize this approach in dealing with IGP models and report successful results. The power of the approach is, of course, directly dependent upon the power of the specific single-objective algorithm (or associated software) as employed in step 3.

Modifications to classical approaches. An alternative approach to IGP is available by the relatively straightforward means of modifying "classical" approaches to integer programming; such as the cutting plane method (Gomory, 1958), branch and bound (Land and Doig, 1960), or the Balas algorithm (Balas, 1965). I developed a number of such algorithms in the late 1960s and early 1970s, some of which appear as Chapter 5 of *Goal Programming and Extensions* (Ignizio, 1976b). In general, however, these modified algorithms have not proven very effective. They have all the limitations and problems associated with their single-objective counterparts and typically only exhibit adequate performance on relatively small to modest size models. Further, because the ultimate performance of the method rests primariliy upon the efficiency of the structure of the algorithms and its coding, it is my opinion that one is better off taking advantage of already developed single-objective IP codes—such as are available via sequential IGP—or the goal aggregation method, as described next.

Goal aggregation. The goal aggregation approach proceeds as follows (Ignizio, 1985b). First, one solves the *relaxed* linear IGP model (i.e., the integer restrictions are ignored). Next, using the shadow price column vectors of the relaxed model's final tableau, we construct a small LP model. The solution to this LP model provides a set of weights by which we may change the linear IGP model into a conventional IP model, and then solve by conventional IP software.

The steps of the goal aggregation algorithm are as follows:

Step 1. Form the linear IGP model.

Step 2. Solve, via any LGP code, the *relaxed* version of the model developed in step 1. If all integer variables are integer valued, stop. Otherwise, delete any deviation variables having $d_j^{(1)} < 0$ and go to step 3.

Step 3. Determine the weights for the modified form by solving the following LP model:

$$\text{minimize } (W_2 - W_K)$$

s.t.

$$\sum_{k=2}^{K} W_k d_j^{(k)} < 0 \qquad \text{for all j nonbasic}$$

$$W_k \geqslant 0 \qquad \text{for all } k \geqslant 2$$

and

$$W_k > W_{k+1} \qquad \text{for all } k \geqslant 2$$

Step 4. Use the weights found in step 3 to convert the linear IGP model into a new, equivalent, linear IP model. That is,

$$\text{lexmin } \mathbf{u}^T = \left\{\mathbf{c}^{(1)T}\mathbf{v},\ \mathbf{c}^{(2)T}\mathbf{v}, \ldots, \mathbf{c}^{(K)T}\mathbf{v}\right\}$$

s.t.

$$\mathbf{Av} = \mathbf{b}$$

$$\mathbf{v} \geqslant \mathbf{0}$$

becomes

$$\text{minimize } W_2\, \mathbf{c}^{(2)T}\mathbf{v} + \ldots + W_K\, \mathbf{c}^{(K)T}\mathbf{v}$$

$$\mathbf{Av} = \mathbf{b}$$

$$\mathbf{v} \geqslant \mathbf{0}$$

Step 5. Solve the model developed in step 4 by any appropriate conventional linear IP algorithm.

To illustrate the approach, consider this example:

$$\text{lexmin } \mathbf{u}^T = \{(\rho_1), (\eta_2), (10\eta_3 + \eta_4)\}$$

$$x_1 + 2x_2 + \eta_1 - \rho_1 = 1$$

$$x_2 + \eta_2 - \rho_2 = 3$$

$$8x_1 + 10x_2 + \eta_3 - \rho_3 = 80$$

$$10x_1 + 8x_2 + \eta_4 - \rho_4 = 80$$

and x_1 and x_2 must be nonnegative *integers*.

The final tableau for the *relaxed* version of this model is given in the following table. Also listed are the shadow price column vectors for each nonbasic variable.

	Basis Inverse				β
$x_2 = v_2$	1/2	0	0	0	1/2
$\eta_2 = v_4$	−1/2	1	0	0	5/2
$\eta_3 = v_5$	−5	0	1	0	75
$\eta_4 = v_6$	−4	0	0	1	76
$\pi^{(1)T}$	0	0	0	0	0
$\pi^{(2)T}$	−1/2	1	0	0	5/2
$\pi^{(3)T}$	−54	0	10	1	826

$$(x_1): \mathbf{d}_1 = \begin{pmatrix} 0 \\ -1/2 \\ 36 \end{pmatrix} \quad (\eta_1): \mathbf{d}_3 = \begin{pmatrix} 0 \\ -1/2 \\ -54 \end{pmatrix} \quad (\rho_1): \mathbf{d}_7 = \begin{pmatrix} -1 \\ 1/2 \\ 54 \end{pmatrix}$$

$$(\rho_2): \mathbf{d}_8 = \begin{pmatrix} 0 \\ -1 \\ 0 \end{pmatrix} \quad (\rho_3): \mathbf{d}_9 = \begin{pmatrix} 0 \\ 0 \\ -10 \end{pmatrix} \quad (\rho_4): \mathbf{d}_{10} = \begin{pmatrix} 0 \\ 0 \\ -1 \end{pmatrix}$$

From step 2 we see we must proceed as not all integer variables have integer values (i.e., $x_2 = 1/2$). Further, ρ_1 (or v_7) must be deleted because $d_7^{(1)} = -1$.

Moving to step 3, our LP model to be solved is as follows:

$$\text{minimize } W_2 - W_3$$

$$\begin{aligned} -1/2\,W_2 + 36\,W_3 &< 0 \\ -1/2\,W_2 - 54\,W_3 &< 0 \\ -\quad W_2 \qquad\quad &< 0 \\ -10\,W_3 &< 0 \\ -\quad W_3 &< 0 \end{aligned}$$

$$W_2,\ W_3 \geqslant 0$$

$$\text{and } W_2 > W_3$$

Although the strict inequality constraints are unusual, we may accommodate them by adding some small negative amount, say ϵ, to the right-hand sides. Thus, we replace < 0 by $\leq \epsilon$. One solution to this model is

$$W_2 = 73 \qquad W_3 = 1$$

Consequently, the aggregated IP model is given as

$$\text{minimize } 73\eta_2 + 10\eta_3 + \eta_4$$

$$\begin{aligned} x_1 + 2x_2 + \eta_1 \qquad &= 1 \\ x_2 + \eta_2 - \rho_2 &= 3 \\ 8x_1 + 10x_2 + \eta_3 - \rho_3 &= 80 \\ 10x_1 + 8x_2 + \eta_4 - \rho_4 &= 80 \end{aligned}$$

and x_1, x_2 are nonnegative integers.

This last model may be solved by any conventional approach to linear IP and the resulting program ($x_1^* = 1$, $x_2^* = 0$) must be optimal for the original IGP models.

Network simplex. Certain conventional integer programming problems may find convenient representation as networks. If so, some very powerful approaches based on network simplex may be used to obtain a solution. Further, the time required to find that solution may be only a fraction of that required by more "conventional" approaches (Glover et al., 1974).

It is also possible to treat certain integer GP problems as networks and then apply an extension of conventional network simplex to develop a solution. Just as in the conventional (i.e., single-objective) case, *when this is possible* the computational efficiency may be considerably enhanced. As such, for those IGP problems that may find such representation, the network simplex approach should certainly be considered (Ignizio, 1983d, 1983f; Ignizio and Daniels, 1983; Price, 1978).

Heuristic programming. Despite years of substantial effort in IP, it is still true that many real world IP or IGP problems are simply too large and/or complex for solution (or at least solution in a reasonable amount of time) by exact methods (Ignizio, 1980a). In such cases we typically resort to specially tailored heuristic methods. With these methods we seek *acceptable* solutions in an acceptable amount of time. The references provide a discussion of some of the uses of heuristic programming in IGP (Harnett and Ignizio, 1973; Ignizio, 1976c, 1979a, 1981d, 1984; Ignizio et al., 1982; Murphy and Ignizio, 1984; Palmer et al., 1982).

Nonlinear GP

Sequential nonlinear goal programming. Using an approach analogous to that described for sequential integer goal programming we could, if we wished, solve nonlinear GP models. However, although this is possible and sometimes done, it is both inefficient and unnecessary in the case of nonlinear GP. The reason for this is that conventional nonlinear programming algorithms and codes may *easily* be modified to handle—*directly*—the nonlinear GP case.

Modifications to classical approaches. The very first approach to nonlinear GP (Ignizio, 1963) was based on the modification of existing, conventional nonlinear programming methods. Specifically, the "pattern search" method of Hooke and Jeeves (1961) was converted into an algorithm and code for nonlinear GP. The success of this result led me to investigate such conversions for virtually all other conventional nonlinear programming algorithms. In most cases, the key change to the conventional code is the simple replacement of the scalar objective function, z, with the achievement *vector*, **u**. For example, a typical search algorithm for conventional nonlinear programming will proceed as follows:

Step 1. Formulate the model and set t = 1 (where t is simply a counter). Determine some trial solution and denote the program and solution as $\mathbf{x}^t$ and z^t.

Step 2. Define a region, or "neighborhood" about $\mathbf{x}^t$ and then determine a direction of improvement, from $\mathbf{x}^t$, within this neighborhood.

Step 3. Determine a "step length" along the direction of improvement found in step 2 and move along this length to a new program, $\mathbf{x}^{t+1}$. Evaluate z^{t+1}.

Step 4. Repeat steps 2 and 3 until one converges to the optimal solution (a result rarely known except for trivial models) or must stop according to certain stopping rules (e.g., too many iterations, lack of significant improvement).

Now, to modify this approach so as to handle NLGP models we may simply replace z^t by $\mathbf{u}^t$ in steps 1 and 3. Modification of most search algorithms to accommodate the resulting evaluation of **u** is typically a minor procedure.

Of the classical algorithms converted, the best results, by far, have been achieved with algorithms based upon:

- pattern search (Hooke and Jeeves, 1961),
- the Gifffith/Stewart technique (1961), and
- generalized reduced gradient methods (Lasdon, 1970).

The results accomplished with the modified pattern search method for NLGP (Draus et al., 1977; Ignizio, 1963, 1976a, 1979b, 1981b; McCammon and Thompson, 1980; Ng, 1981) have been particularly impressive. Engineering design problems (e.g., phased arrays, transducer design) with thousands of variables and hundreds of rows are routinely solved with the latest versions of NLGP/PS (i.e., nonlinear GP via modified pattern search). Further, not only are such problems of large size, they are also typically of high density (in fact, densities of 100% are not uncommon). Although such densities alone typically defeat simplex based nonlinear algorithms, the NLGP/PS codes are relatively unaffected.

Interactive GP

In the past several years there has been, in some quarters, an intense interest in so-called interactive methods for decision support. (Gass and Dror, 1983; Ignizio, 1979a, 1979b, 1981a, 1981d, 1982a, 1983c; Ignizio et al., 1982; Khorramshahgol and Ignizio, 1984; Masud and Hwang, 1981). By interactive, it is meant that one encourages and utilizes certain direct support of the decision maker in actually solving the decision model. Such approaches have received particularly favorable reviews by many of those in the fields of multicriteria decision making (MCDM) and multiobjective mathematical programming.

Included among the interactive approaches proposed are a number that require the decision maker to sit in front of a CRT (i.e., monitor) and react to a set of alternatives. That is, he or she indicates the most (or, perhaps, least) preferred alternative from a small group of alternatives. Using this information, the procedure moves to a new group of alternatives and again the decision maker is asked to respond. It is hoped that with the input provided by the decision maker, such a procedure will lead to either the "optimal" result or at least one that is acceptable.

Unfortunately—at least for those who would hope to use such methods on real problems with real decision makers—many of these interactive methods are based on a rather naive view of the world and, in particular, of real-world decision makers. That is, it is (at least from my experience) rare to find a chief executive officer who is willing to even take the time to be shown how such methods work, much less spend the time required to provide the necessary interaction. It is for these reasons that (successful) interactive versions of GP typically are designed to minimize the time and effort required of the busy decision maker. To clarify, we shall present just one interactive GP approach, the technique known as "augmented GP" (Ignizio, 1979a, 1979b, 1981a, 1981d, 1982a, 1983c; Ignizio et al., 1982).

Augmented GP proceeds as if one were, at first, simply solving a GP model. That is, the initial input required of the decision maker is as follows:

(1) estimates as to the aspiration levels as required to convert all objectives (of the baseline model) into goals, and

(2) estimates as to the order of the importance of all goals.

A solution to this initial GP model is then derived and presented to the decision maker(s) as a "candidate solution." Now, when dealing with any nontrivial real-world problem subject to multiple (and conflicting) objectives, any solution developed represents a compromise. Consequently, some goals may be completely achieved whereas others are relatively far from achievement. Thus, if the candidate solution is considered unacceptable, the next step in the procedure is to ask that the decision maker indicate just how much he or she would allow each goal to be degraded if such degradation would result in some substantial improvement to another goal or goals. The indication of these degradations then defines a "region of acceptable degradation." We next develop a subset of the efficient (i.e., nondominated) solutions in this region and present this subset to the decision maker.

If any member of the subset is acceptable, we may stop. Otherwise, in examining this subset the decision maker can get a fairly good idea as to how much impact the degradation of one goal will have on the others. For example, the decision maker may find the cost of a candidate solution acceptable but may not be pleased with, say, the resultant system reliability. However, if he or she notes that cost must be drastically increased to produce even a small increase in reliability, this information may well result in the decision maker accepting some previously rejected earlier candidate solution.

For those readers desiring further references (and examples of implementation) on augmented GP, we suggest the following references: Ignizio (1979a, 1979b, 1981a, 1981d, 1982a, 1983c) and Ignizio et al. (1982).

NOTES

1. Huss, in fact, considered the results so transparent as to not warrant even an attempt at publication. However, in recent years sequential GP has become the focus of some rather intense, although belated, interest.

2. For lexicographic LGP, to be precise.

3. This specific model is also a special case of the more general form of mathematical programming model known as the MULTIPLEX model (Ignizio, forthcoming).

4. The symbol $\forall$ denotes "for all."

5. In equation 3.3 only one of the relations ($\leq$, =, or $\geq$) is assumed to hold for each t.

6. Where, again, only one of the relations ($\leq$, =, or $\geq$) holds for each i.

7. Using the transformed form of the LGP model, the reader should be able to prove easily that the *program* (i.e., **v**) for an LGP model can itself be unbounded but, of course, $\mathbf{u}^T$ will be finite. Further, standard pivoting rules preclude a pivot to an unbounded program (i.e., some $v_j \rightarrow \infty$).

8. In actual practice, and in the algorithm to follow, there is no need to generate but *one* element of each d_j for each iteration.

9. Numerous approaches for accomplishing step 7 have been described. Our approach, to be described in the example to follow, uses the "explicit form of the inverse."

10. Note that $r_{B,i}$ is the upper bound on the ith basic variable. Further, $\beta_i = v_{B,i}$.

11. Note, however, that the column check operation of continuous LGP is not permitted here if any variables are restricted to be integers.

12. Where "$\cup$" denotes the union operator.

REFERENCES

ANDERSON, A. M. and M. D. EARLE (1983) "Diet planning in the Third World by linear and goal programming." Journal of the Operational Research Society 34: 9-13.

BALAS, E. (1965) "An additive algorithm for solving linear programs with zero-one variables." Operations Research 13: 517-546.

BRES, E. S., D. BURNS, A. CHARNES, and W. W. COOPER (1980) "A goal programming model for planning officer accessions." Management Science 26: 773-783.

CAMPBELL, H. and J. P. IGNIZIO (1972) "Using linear programming for predicting student performance." Journal of Educational and Psychological Measurement 32: 397-401.

CHARNES, A. and W. W. COOPER (1977) "Goal programming and multiple objective optimizations." European Journal of Operational Research 1: 307-322.

———(1975) "Goal programming and constrained regression—a comment." OMEGA 3: 403-409.

———(1961) Management Models and Industrial Applications of Linear Programming (vols. 1 and 2). New York: John Wiley.

———and R. FERGUSON (1955) "Optimal executive compensation by linear programming." Management Science 1: 138-151.

CHARNES, A., W. W. COOPER, K. R. KARWAN, and W. A. WALLACE (1979) "A chance constrained goal programming model for resource allocation in a marine environmental protection program." Journal of Environmental Economy and Management 6: 244-274.

———(1976) "A goal interval programming model for resource allocation in a marine environmental protection program." Journal of Environmental Economy and Management 3: 347-362.

CHARNES, A., W. W. COOPER, D. KLINGMAN, and R. J. NIEHAUS (1975) "Explicit solutions in convex goal programming." Management Science 22: 438-448.

CLAYTON, E. R., W. E. WEBER, and B. W. TAYLOR (1982) "A goal programming approach to the optimization of multiresponse simulation models." IIE Transactions 14: 282-287.

COOK, W. D. (1984) "Goal programming and financial planning models for highway rehabilitation." Journal of the Operational Research Society 35: 217-224.

DANTZIG, G. B. (1982) "Reminiscences about the origins of linear programming." Operations Research Letters 1: 43-48.

DE KLUYVER, C. A. (1979) "An exploration of various goal programming formulations—with application to advertising media scheduling." Journal of the Operational Research Society 30: 161-171.

———(1978) "Hard and soft constraints in media scheduling." Journal of Advertising Research 18: 27-31.

DRAUS, S. M., J. P. IGNIZIO, and G. L. WILSON (1977, June) "The design of optimum sonar transducer arrays using goal programming." Proceedings of the 93rd meeting of the Acoustical Society of America, University Park, Pennsylvania.

FRAZER, J. R. (1968) Applied Linear Programming. Englewood Cliffs, NJ: Prentice-Hall.

FREED, N. and F. GLOVER (1981) "Simple but powerful goal programming models for discriminant problems." European Journal of Operational Research 7: 44-60.

GARROD, N. W. and B. MOORES (1978) "An implicit enumeration algorithm for solving zero-one goal programming problems." OMEGA 6: 374-377.

GASS, S. I. and M. DROR (1983) "An interactive approach to multiple-objective linear programming involving key decision variables." Large Scale Systems 5: 95-103.

GLOVER, F., D. KARNEY, and D. KLINGMAN (1974) "Implementation and computational comparisons of primal, dual, and primal-dual computer codes for minimum cost network flow problems." Networks 4: 192-211.

GOMORY, R. E. (1958) "Outline of an algorithm for integer solutions to linear programs." Bulletin of the American Mathematical Society 64: 275-278.

GRIFFITH, R. E. and R. A. STEWART (1961) "A nonlinear programming technique for the optimization of continuous processing systems." Management Science 7: 379-392.

HARNETT, R. M. and P. IGNIZIO (1973) "A heuristic program for the covering problem with multiple objectives," in R. Cochrane and M. Zeleny (eds.) Multiple Criteria Decision Making. Columbia: University of South Carolina Press.

HOOKE, R. and T. A. JEEVES (1961) "Direct search solution of numerical and statistical problems." Journal of the Association of Computing Machinery 8: 212-229.

IGNIZIO, J. P. (forthcoming) "Multiobjective mathematical programming via the MULTIPLEX model and algorithm." European Journal of Operational Research.

———(1985a) "An algorithm for the linear goal program dual." Journal of the Operational Research Society 36: 507-515.

———(1985b) "Integer GP via goal aggregation." Large Scale Systems 8: 81-86.

———(1984) "A generalized goal programming approach to the minimal interference, multicriteria N × 1 scheduling problem." Institute for Industrial Engineering Transactions, Atlanta 16: 316-322.

———(1983a) "Convergence properties of the multiphase of simplex algorithm for goal programming." Advances in Management Studies 2: 311-333.

———(ed.) (1983b) Generalized Goal Programming. New York: Pergamon.

———(1983c) "Generalized goal programming: an overview." Computers and Operations Research 10: 277-290.

———(1983d) "An approach to the modeling and analysis of multiobjective generalized networks." European Journal of Operational Research 12: 357-361.

———(1983e) "A note on computational methods in lexicographic linear goal programming." Journal of the Operational Research Society 34: 539-542.

———(1983f) "GP-GN: an approach to certain large-scale multiobjective integer programming models." Large Scale Systems 4: 177-188.

———(1982a) Linear Programming in Single and Multiple Objective Systems. Englewood Cliffs, NJ: Prentice-Hall.

———(1982b) "On the rediscovery of fuzzy goal programming." Decision Sciences 13: 331-336.

———(1981a) "The determination of a subset of efficient solutions via goal programming." Computers and Operations Research 8: 9-16.

———(1981b) "Antenna array beam pattern synthesis via goal programming." European Journal of Operational Research 6: 286-290.

———(1981c, May) "Goal programming and IE." Proceedings II Symposia Internacional de Ingenieria Industrial, Nogales, Mexico.

———(1981d, December) "Capital budgeting via interactive GP." Proceedings of the American Institute for Industrial Engineering, Washington, DC.

———(1980a) "Solving large-scale problems: a venture into a new dimension." Journal of the Operational Research Society 31: 217-225.

———(1980b) "An introduction to goal programming with applications in urban systems." Computers, Environment and Urban Systems 5: 15-34.

———(1979a) "Goal programming and large scale network design." Proceedings Annual Review of Distributed Processing (U.S. Army Ballistical Missile Defense Advanced Technical Center, St. Petersburg, FL).

———(1979b) "Extension of goal programming." Proceedings of the American Institute for Decision Sciences, New Orleans.

———(1979c) "Multiobjective capital budgeting and fuzzy programming." Proceedings of the American Institute for Industrial Engineering, Houston.

———(1978) "The development of cost estimating relationships via goal programming." Engineering Economist 24: 37-47.

———(1978b) "Goal programming: a tool for multiobjective analysis." Journal of the Operational Research Society 29: 1109-1119.

———(1977) "Curve and response surface fitting by goal programming." Proceedings of Pittsburgh Conference on Modeling and Simulation (April): 1091-1093.

———(1976a) "The modeling of systems having multiple measures of effectiveness."

Proceedings of Pittsburgh Conference on Modeling and Simulation (April): 572-576.
———(1976b) Goal Programming and Extensions. Lexington, MA: D. C. Heath.
———(1976c) "An approach to the capital budgeting problem with multiple objectives." Engineering Economist 22: 259-272.
———(1974a) The Development of the Multidimensional Dual in Linear Goal Programming. Working paper, Pennsylvania State University.
———(1974b) A Primal-Dual Algorithm for Linear Goal Programming. Working paper, Pennsylvania State University.
———(1967) "A FORTRAN code for multiple objective LP." Internal memorandum, North American Aviation Corporation, Downey, CA.
———(1963) S-II Trajectory Study and Optimum Antenna Placement. Report SID-63, North American Aviation Corporation, Downey, CA.
———and J. H. PERLIS (1979) "Sequential linear goal programming: implementation via MPSX." Computers and Operations Research 6: 141-145.
IGNIZIO, J. P. and S. C. DANIELS (1983) "Fuzzy multicriteria integer programming via fuzzy generalized networks." Fuzzy Sets and Systems 10: 261-270.
IGNIZIO, J. P. and D. E. SATTERFIELD (1977) "Antenna array beam pattern synthesis via goal programming." Military Electronics Defense (September): 402-417.
IGNIZIO, J. P. and L. C. THOMAS (1984) "An enhanced conversion scheme for lexicographic multiobjective integer programming." European Journal of Operational Research 18: 57-61.
IGNIZIO, J. P., D. PALMER, and C. A. MURPHY (1982) "A multicriteria approach to the overall design of supersystems." Institute for Electrical and Electronic Engineering Transactions on Computers C-31: 410-418.
IJIRI, Y. (1965) Management Goals and Accounting for Control. Chicago: Rand-McNally.
JAASKELAINEN, V. (1976) Linear Programming and Budgeting. New York: Petrocelli-Charter.
———(1969) Accounting and Mathematical Programming. Helsinki School of Economics.
KEOWN, A. J. and B. W. TAYLOR (1980) "A chance constrained integer goal programming model for capital budgeting in the production area." Journal of the Operational Research Society 31: 579-589.
KHORRAMSHAHGOL, R. and J. P. IGNIZIO (1984) Single and Multiple Decision Making in a Multiple Objective Environment. Working paper, Pennsylvania State University.
KNOLL, A. L. and A. ENGELBERG (1978) "Weighting multiple objectives—the Churchman-Ackoff Technique revisited." Computers and Operations Research 5: 165-177.
KORNBLUTH, J.S.H. (1973) "A survey of goal programming." OMEGA 1: 193-205.
LAND, A. H. and A. G. DOIG (1960) "An automatic method of solving discrete programming problems." Econometrica 28: 497-520.
LASDON, L. S. (1970) Optimization Theory for Large Systems. London: Macmillan.
MARKOWSKI, C. A. and J. P. IGNIZIO (1983a) "Theory and properties of the lexicographic linear goal programming dual." Large Scale Systems 5: 115-122.
———(1983b) "Duality and transformations in multiphase and sequential LGP." Computers and Operations Research 10: 321-334.
MASUD, A. S. and C. L. HWANG (1981) "Interactive sequential goal programming." Journal of the Operational Research Society 32: 391-400.

McCAMMON, D. F. and W. THOMPSON, Jr. (1980) "The design of Tonpilz piezoelectric transducers using nonlinear goal programming." Journal of the Acoustical Society of America 68: 754-757.

MOORE, L. J., B. W. TAYLOR, E. R. CLAYTON, and S. M. LEE (1978) "An analysis of a multicriteria project crashing model." AIIE Transactions 10: 163-169.

MORRIS, W. T. (1964) The Analysis of Management Decisions. Homewood, IL: Richard D. Irwin.

MURPHY, C. M. and J. P. IGNIZIO (1984) "A methodology for multicriteria network partitioning." Computers and Operations Research 11: 1-12.

MURTAGH, B. A. (1981) Advanced Linear Programming. New York: McGraw-Hill.

NG, K.Y.K (1981) "Solution of Navier-Stokes equations by goal programming." Journal of Computational Physics 39: 103-111.

PALMER, D., J. P. IGNIZIO, and C. A. MURPHY (1982) "Optimal design of distributed supersystems." Proceedings of the National Computer Conference, pp. 193-198.

PERLIS, J. H. and J. P. IGNIZIO (1983) "Stability analysis: an approach to the evaluation of system design." Cybernetics and Systems 11: 87-103.

POURAGHABAGHER, A. R. (1983, November) "Application of goal programming in shop scheduling." Presented at the ORSA/TIMS meeting, Orlando, Florida.

PRICE, W. L. (1978) "Solving goal programming manpower models using advanced network codes." Journal of the Operational Research Society 29: 1231-1239.

SUTCLIFFE, C., J. BOARD, and P. CHESHIRE (1984) "Goal programming and allocating children to secondary schools in reading." Journal of Operational Research Society 35: 719-730.

TAYLOR, B. W., L. J. MOORE, and E. R. CLAYTON (1982) "R & D project selection and manpower allocation with integer nonlinear goal programming." Management Science 28: 1149-1158.

WILSON, G. L. and J. P. IGNIZIO (1977, summer) "The use of computers in the design of sonar arrays." Proceedings of the 9th International Congress on Acoustics, Madrid.

YU, P. L. (1973) "Introduction to domination structures in multicriteria problems." Proceedings of seminar on multiple criteria decision making, University of South Carolina, Columbia.

ZANAKIS, S. H. and M. W. MARET (1981) "A Markovian goal programming approach to aggregate manpower planning." Journal of the Operational Research Society 32: 55-63.

ZIMMERMANN, H.-J. (1978) "Fuzzy programming and linear programming with several objectives." Fuzzy Sets and Systems 1: 45-55.

JAMES P. IGNIZIO is Professor of Industrial and Management Systems Engineering at the Pennsylvania State University. He is the author of four books, several monographs, and over 150 technical papers and reports. He has been actively engaged in the research, development, and application of goal programming (and other multiple objective methods) since 1962. Dr. Ignizio is also recipient of the First Hartford Prize and a Fellow of the Operational Research Society.